DISCERNMENT

DISCERNMENT

THE BUSINESS
ATHLETE'S
REGIMEN FOR
A GREAT LIFE
THROUGH BETTER
DECISIONS

JEFF DUDAN

the will to win ™
media group

DISCERNMENT
The Business Athlete's Regimen for a Great
Life through Better Decisions

ISBN   978-1-5445-0852-8 *Hardcover*
         978-1-5445-0850-4 *Paperback*
         978-1-5445-0851-1 *Ebook*
         978-1-5445-1457-4 *Audiobook*

To my wife Traci and children Zack, Maelee, and Jack.

May we grow older and wiser together.

CONTENTS

INTRODUCTION

I went to college on a football scholarship, and without it, I might not have completed my education. Even with it, I needed to hold down a job. Before I left home, I'd worked as everything from a furniture mover to the dog at Chuck E. Cheese. All work is honorable, but trust me on this: Some jobs are better than others. At college, I started my first company with my roommate painting student apartments. We grew the business, taught it to other guys, and eventually handed it off to our brothers. From there, I started a restoration company that I grew, franchised, and sold. I've generated hundreds of millions of dollars of enterprise value in the businesses I've built. It's enabled me to make a meaningful impact on thousands of lives and create a legacy for future generations of my family.

In my years of grinding to build my businesses, and in helping others do the same, I've come to recognize similarities in those who play the game of business well—and it is a game. Score is kept, and there are winners and losers. Great business athletes

- Train on the fundamentals and never stop learning.
- Push themselves to compete and reach the next level.
- Strive to lead their team and carry the ball.
- Perform. When the lights go up, they show up. All the world is a stage for business athletes, and they want to star.

Finally, business athletes seek out great coaching. If you want to get to the major leagues in business, you'll need a coach. Here's why I'm the man for the job, at least for the next hundred or so pages.

I've made some good decisions. Marrying my wife was probably the best, but I've been featured on the TV show *Undercover Boss*, and I'm chair of the fastest-growing YPO chapter in the world. I've studied, thought, and read a lot about business, and I never quit sports. I've coached football, baseball, and basketball, and dovetailing commerce and coaching has made me a stronger business athlete and more effective at training others.

When I coach young people, I tell my players that they'll face ninety-nine choices each day, starting with whether to make their beds and what to eat for breakfast. These small decisions, and all the bigger ones they make, will impact their world, their circumstances, and their outcomes, and those of the people around them.

Young people are no less intelligent than adults, but they are less experienced, and as a result, their decisions are less informed. Wisdom is the accumulation of knowledge over time, and discernment is its application to a present situation. At its simplest, discernment is the ability to make appropriate decisions—at a particular moment in space and time—well.

Decision-making is a full-contact sport, and the farther up the org chart you go, the more impact your decisions have. I've met plenty of people who didn't step up to leadership roles precisely because they didn't want to shoulder the burden of making sink-or-swim decisions that critically impacted other people. Whether you're starting a side hustle or climbing your way up the corporate ladder, it takes courage to make high-stakes choices with possibly far-reaching bad outcomes for you, your company, and your people. It's not easy. Sometimes there are no good options, and often there's not enough information. Outcomes are rarely certain ahead of time.

High-level decisions are educated guesses about probable outcomes. Discernment is critical, but not because it ensures total control over end results. It doesn't. Business is a probabilities game. Discernment allows you to understand and reduce (if not eliminate) the downside risks of a decision while simultaneously choosing the path most likely to get you where you'd most like to go.

When I coach football, I break the game down into skills and build training drills around them. To train your discernment, we'll first need a breakdown of what discernment really is. Football, stripped down, is blocking and tackling. *Discernment, at its core, is a principled, effective, experience-informed process for powerful decision-making.*

Discernment is a word people use to mean everything from having good judgment to having awareness without judgment, but the definition I've just given is more to our purposes. It's one I've come to during my years of practice, experience, and study—one that we'll explore, word by word, in the chapters that follow.

When I coach, the first thing I do with my players is build consensus around the kind of team they want to be. In this book, we'll start the same way. Chapter 1, "Learn Your Game," will establish exactly what we're going to accomplish in our time together by describing what discernment looks like in action.

Once you know the game you're playing, we'll start working

a program to develop the component parts. I've said discernment is principled and effective. To be principled, you need to build strong core values, and to be effective, you must have a game plan. In Chapters 2 and 3, I'll show you how to define what matters most to you, and I'll give you guidelines for setting your most crucial goals.

Discernment is based in experience, so I'll walk you through ways to increase your exposure to business fundamentals in Chapter 4 and discuss how to develop your unique abilities in Chapter 5.

For your decisions to be powerful, you need to be mentally, physically, emotionally, and intellectually fit, and because teams compound power, you need to learn to lead. I'll train your fitness and leadership in Chapters 6 and 7, respectively. Finally, to make sure these components of discernment work in concert, the last skill we'll develop is the meta-skill of establishing a training cadence and discernment-advancing habits.

I want to help you recognize great opportunities for learning and growth, understand their value, and know what to do when they appear, but this isn't an inspirational book. Just reading it won't change your life. Only your hard work can do that, so practice what you learn. It's on you to put in the hours.

This isn't a new scholarly management system book either.

I've read a lot of research-based leadership and personal development books, and what I've learned will inform what I recommend, but I haven't conducted a bunch of experiments on anyone but myself. I have, however, made a meaningful impact on the lives of others (and multiple millions) by breaking down the skills of success and training hard on them. I'll share my regimen for creating a great life through better decision-making as well as some illustrative stories from my personal journey.

I was an athlete before I was a business athlete, and I believe bringing the principles of that early training with me into my business life contributed to my success. Even if you've never played a sport, you'll perform better in life if you adopt the training mindset. But before you get out on the field, you have to know what game you're playing, and that's where we'll start—by gaining deeper insight into what discernment is and why it matters.

CHAPTER 1

LEARN YOUR GAME

SPOTTING DISCERNMENT IN ACTION

In 1992, I was living in Boone, North Carolina, running a painting business I'd started as a student at Appalachian State University. The company was doing well, and I was dating the woman I would eventually marry when I made a decision to pack up my truck and drive to Florida to help with cleanup after Hurricane Andrew. It was a "fork in the road" moment, but like many high-impact decisions, its wisdom became clear only in hindsight. At the time, the decision was made mostly because it sounded like an adventure.

It was ultimately a good decision, but I don't recall giving it much careful thought. I was a young man, and while I still think the instinct to move toward adventure rather than the sofa is a good one, at the time I was picking my path more by inclination than deliberation. Still, every decision is ultimately a choice. In the immortal words of Geddy Lee, "When you choose not to decide, you still have made a choice." Decisions are inevitable; discernment isn't.

Discernment is like a personality. Just because you have one doesn't mean it's any good. But the quality of your decisions determines the quality of your life, so I want to show you what discernment looks like in action.

Think about it like this: You train kids to play a sport by breaking it down into a set of skills—you pitch, you dribble, you run, you bunt, you shoot, you pass. But if the kids haven't seen the game played, they won't know when to do what. Learning to identify discernment is the step before the first step. In other words, you need to know what you want to achieve before you set out to accomplish it.

> The quality of your decisions determines the quality of your life.

Once I decided to go to Florida, I jumped in my truck and headed south. During the whole drive down, everything looked normal until I came over a rise on I-95 South near Hallandale. I'll never forget the way the entire landscape changed. Behind me was an ordinary world. In front of me was tragedy. Not a single building I could see had a roof.

Trees had been sandblasted barkless, yachts sat smashed on the road, and a big-box store gaped without a roof or walls, its exposed beams like the twisted roots of fallen trees. I drove by destroyed home after destroyed home thinking about the people who'd lived regular lives there just the week before. It was hard to imagine how anything could ever be the same for those families again.

By the time I got to Homestead, I'd driven two hours through that level of devastation, and I knew I was staying. I threw in with my friend Clint and started doing emergency cleanup and demolition—drying in roofs, helping people protect their property—while learning to play the insurance restoration game. It was baptism by fire, and I picked up decades of knowledge in seventeen short, intense months. I learned how to re-roof skyscrapers, restore mansions, and rebuild thousand-unit apartment complexes, and how to navigate insurance coverages, negotiate multimillion-dollar settlements, and collect payment.

As the recovery work was winding down, my buddy Tom and I had a meeting with two guys we'd met in the course of our work. They were a decade or so older than we were and had master's degrees from the University of Florida in building construction. We admired them and were eager to learn from their experience and to benefit from their resumes. In us, I imagine they saw two guys with plenty of hustle and young backs. We decided to go into business together doing insurance repairs and reconstruction.

The cost of entry was $5,000 each, and I didn't have the cash, so I drove the twelve hours back to North Carolina. I took my paint-splotched, four-cylinder truck down to the local bank and negotiated a $5,000 loan on it. My brother Mike was running the painting business by then, so I handed the payment book to him. I told him, "When you get it paid off, this is your truck," and I drove back to Florida with my fourth of our startup capital ready to take on the world.

When I got there, I learned the older guys were planning to split 51 percent of the company between them and divide the remaining 49 percent between Tom and me. They were our mentors and had much more experience plus advanced degrees, but even then, I knew what that one percentage point meant. It meant Tom and I wouldn't have an equal say in the decision-making. I didn't want that, but I couldn't find a good business reason to fight it. Instead, I offered them a trade. I knew how they felt about their alma mater, so I said that if we were all equal partners, we could brand the company with Florida Gator colors. That's how AdvantaClean ended up orange and blue, and how I ended up with a full quarter of it.

It turned out to have been a smart move as soon as just a year later, when three of us bought the fourth guy out. By

2004, I owned the company outright. They were all good guys and hard workers, but I had a vision of AdvantaClean as a national company and was pushing us to try new things and to invest more in the brand. My partners each decided to take the buyout instead of the gamble. Even the last of them, whose share of the company cost me the most, still made fractions of a cent for every dollar I did when I sold the company in 2019.

This is a story about discernment, but its moral isn't that I had the discernment to know AdvantaClean would eventually be as valuable as it was. I didn't. I did know it would always be about people. People were the reason I traded Gator colors for half of one percentage point—I wanted us to all be equal partners. People were the reason I bought my partners out. Had we stayed together, they wouldn't be any richer now than they are. In any alternate scenario that included them, AdvantaClean would never have franchised. It wouldn't have grown as quickly or made as much. If we're practicing spotting discernment in action, what you should pay attention to here is the wisdom captured in the expression "Show me your friends, and I'll show you your future."

> Show me your friends, and I'll show you your future.

You're going to make a lot of decisions in your life, and they aren't all going to be great. Not every swing is a hit, and that's fine. Sometimes, you'll have to choose between two bad options. Sometimes, you won't have enough information or time to make an informed choice. Sometimes, you'll just whiff. None of that matters. What matters is your average over time. If you're batting under 50 percent—making more poor decisions than good ones—it's going to negatively impact your life, your business, and everyone around you. Educating yourself and training your discernment improve the probability that you'll increasingly make more right choices than wrong ones.

I first learned this from a man who'd retired as the CFO of Pepsi Corporation. When I met him in 2007, he was an elderly guy at the end of his career looking for something to do, so I hired him. It was a terrific opportunity for me to learn from a guy who'd had a long career in a high-level position at an international company. "Jeff," he told me, "nothing is 100 percent. There are no absolutes, just probabilities."

My experience since has proved him out. There's no scenario where you, as a business athlete, are going to have total control over the outcome of the decisions you make. You collect as much data as you can get, create leverage wherever you can, and use all the skills you have to create the scenario that has the highest probability of delivering the results you want. But you do so knowing you can't control for every possibility or predict anything with total confidence.

As an example, in 2017, the company had a chance to be on the TV show *Undercover Boss*. The opportunity came out of nowhere and we had very little time to decide, and so I sat my wife and kids down to get a verdict on whether or not it was something we wanted to do. We're a very private family, and "Be humble" is second on our family's list of values. There was nothing in how we lived our lives that indicated the size of the business we owned. In fact, when I ran football practice in the large side yard of the AdvantaClean building, people would ask me, "So the company lets you practice here. You must know someone, huh?" And I'd just agree that I did. *Undercover Boss*, I knew, would change that, and I warned the kids that people at school might treat them differently too.

I also knew that it could go badly for the company. *Undercover Boss* isn't a documentary. They're looking for good TV, and that means drama and controversy. I was confident that all our franchise owners were aligned with the company's values and that the cameras were only going to "catch" them and their employees doing the right things to the best of their abilities. Still, we would have absolutely no input or say in how the final product came out. We wouldn't even get a sneak preview. We would see the show for the first time with the rest of the world.

The family sat down on the sofa to talk over the decision directly beneath the phrase "Always Do More Than Is Expected," which is emblazoned on our living room wall in huge letters. It's a nod to Jerry Moore, the longtime football coach at Appalachian State University who would routinely scribble this phrase above his signature. We tested the *Undercover Boss* opportunity against our family values, which, in addition to "Be humble," include "Live fun" and "Trust yourself to take chances." With our values leading the way, we decided to do the show, and when it aired, we watched it (a little nervously) along with seven million other viewers. Our episode still runs internationally, and I can tell every time it does by the influx of new social media connections and messages. The show went well, and I'm glad we did it. It ended up being good for the company, and it was an immeasurable learning experience, but we had no way of knowing what the outcome would be.

Filming *Undercover Boss*

Undercover Boss Disguise

You can't always guarantee the outcomes in life, and often you can't even control the inputs. You will almost always make your decisions with incomplete information. While you should never stop seeking more data, time kills deals. Moreover, some risks never show up in the numbers. Particularly as an entrepreneur, you're going to find that numbers may not be available to give you everything you need. After all, if decision-making were completely numbers-driven, we'd have computers do it. You can't always quantify the human element. Humanity is incredible...it's the people who create the variation.

> Nothing is 100 percent. There are no absolutes, just probabilities.

It's easy to see the difference between a right decision and a stupid one, but much harder to know the difference between a right decision and one that's almost right. Discernment is in that margin, in the gap between the numbers. It's the weight of your thumb on the scale of probability. And that's what matters.

THE USUAL PROCESS

The factory-preset human decision-making process follows a simple set of rules. When faced with a decision about how to do something, we

1. Do it the same way we've always done it unless we haven't, in which case...
2. We do it the way other people do it unless nobody's done it before, and then...
3. We do what the numbers tell us to or...
4. We make stuff up.

When I bought out the three guys I'd started AdvantaClean with, it wasn't something I'd always done, it wasn't what most people did, and it certainly wasn't what the numbers dictated—even my father-in-law told me it couldn't work. Nothing justified my decision. But my experience at that point had given me the discernment to believe it was the right one.

A BETTER PROCESS

To say business is all about probabilities means something more profound than it may seem on the surface. It means there are multiple possible outcomes. You can't think, "If X, then Y" anymore. You have to think, "If X, then Y, or Z, or Starfish." This is a much more complex landscape to think your way through. What if X is more probable than Starfish, but Y is preferable to X? Some possible outcomes will be more probable than others. Some will be bad, some good, and some better. A good decision-making process, then, needs to evaluate these multiple possibilities by those two measures: probability and desirability. Your job is to make the most desirable outcome the most probable. To do this, you need to make accurate predictions.

You make predictions based on two things: 1) what you know and 2) what you can imagine.

First, ask yourself: "What is everything I know telling me?"

This includes your gut instincts, your research, your experiences, good data, and the perspectives of other people. It narrows down the field of possibilities you'll consider to the most probable outcomes, taking into account anything that doesn't conflict with your values or the laws of physics. Then you run scenarios on those.

Business athletes read scenarios, not rules.

A scenario is like a little movie you make in your head that lets you "see" the futures that would result from different choices. You ask yourself: "If I do X, what is the most likely scenario?" In other words, how do you think it's most probable that the future would play out if you did X? You imagine the most likely scenarios that might result from X and see how you like them. Then you do the same thing modeling a different choice: "If I do Y, what might happen?"

If probable outcomes for decision X include one good one, one mediocre one, and one that's bad, but the scenarios for decision Y include one fantastic one, one great one, and one that's completely unacceptable, you can't choose Y unless you can reduce the probability of the unacceptable outcome to near zero. Business owners are constantly managing risk and reward. You want rewards as large as possible with the least risk you can manage.

Business athletes develop the ability to assess this quickly.

Leaders who can simultaneously examine multiple scenarios and weigh all the potential consequences in real time bring incredible value to the organizations they lead.

The guys I bought out ran their options—take the money now or hold onto their stake in the company—and they ran the probable outcome scenarios. I would guess these included everything from "Jeff takes crazy risks and runs the company into the ground and I end up with nothing" to "I take the buyout now and later realize I would have made more by staying in." They placed their bets on the probability that the outcome would be closer to the former than the latter.

Business athletes read scenarios, not rules.

The last guy I bought out was a decade older than I was, and he'd been a mentor to me, but we wanted different things for the company. We'd just done about $4.2 million worth of business in ninety days after three hurricanes crisscrossed Florida. There was cash available, but the company had taken out some loans and had other debts outstanding that I would have to take on. The day I signed the paperwork, I went about $4 million into debt. But it was still a good decision, and I'd made it well.

I said in the Introduction that discernment is "a principled, effective, experience-informed process for powerful decision-making." This is what it looks like in action: My decision to buy out the last of my partners wasn't about having total control—that wouldn't have been principled. I paid each of them a fair price (and took on some risk to do it), but I wasn't going to keep doing things the way we'd been doing them just to keep my friends comfortable. That wouldn't have been effective. It was a decision I made by choice, not something I defaulted into, and it was powerful to the tune of quite a large chunk of change by the time I took my own buyout. Finally, it was experience-informed. I'd crammed decades of experience into the seventeen hellish, post-Andrew months, and I already knew the importance of having the right people around me. My coaches, mentors, and friends had shown me my future.

CHAPTER SUMMARY

The quality of your decisions determines the quality of your life, but most people get very little formal training in spotting—much less acquiring—the discernment necessary to make high-quality decisions. Since the cumulative impact of your decisions is so crucial to your ability to both survive and flourish, it's important to understand the role probability plays in decisions, and the common and better processes by which they can be vetted.

CHAPTER 2

STRENGTHEN YOUR CORE

VALUES ARE AT DISCERNMENT'S CORE

My decision to buy out my partners showed discernment because it was based on a better-than-usual process and on a desire to increase my exposure to great people. To make such a determination, I needed to know what "better" and "great" meant to me. "Better" and "great" are value judgments, and if I hadn't had strong core values and been clear about what they were, my discernment wouldn't have had the power to drive that decision.

I bought out my partners because I'd seen the impact the right people could have on my life, and I was hungry to bring new people with different areas of expertise to my table. I'd also seen the impact a business could have on people. I'd seen it on my brother.

While I was starting my painting business in North Carolina, my younger brother, Mike, was back in Schaumburg, Illinois, going to the same junior college I'd gone to and playing football. In his first game, he threw a block that pancaked the other player flat but ripped out Mike's shoulder. Without the means or motivation to get it fixed, my brother's football career was over.

He was taking classes and detailing cars at a car dealership when I suggested he come out for the summer to work with me and get a North Carolina driver's license to establish in-state residency. A year later, he enrolled at Appalachian State and moved into a house I owned, which he managed in lieu of rent. When I left to do disaster recovery in Florida, Mike took over the painting business and put himself through college with it. Here's the lesson I learned from that: I can create a business. I can set it all up and figure it all out. I can get customers, hire people, and lead a team. I can grow that business, and I can give it to somebody else and teach it to them, and they can change their life with it. Mike leveraged that opportunity, earned an accounting degree, and went on to become CFO of the NFL's Carolina Panthers.

Because I valued the transformative power of running a business, the first major management decision I made as AdvantaClean's sole owner was to bring in a consulting company. In the process of working with them to hammer out a purpose, vision, mission, and values statement for the company, I learned about strategy for the first time. We formalized a disaster response plan, and based on it, I poured time and money into building an entire mobile disaster response fleet. When Katrina hit in 2005, we were ready.

Just three months after the storm, AdvantaClean had secured long-term contracts and converted a 12,000-square-foot warehouse into a command center immediately across Lake Pontchartrain from New Orleans. We had everything set up, but my family was still in North Carolina. By this point, my wife and I had three children, and at seven, our oldest, Zack, was about to start his first football season. AdvantaClean was poised to do $50 million worth of work in New Orleans over the next several years (and we did), but I was positioned to be away from my family most of that time.

I knew what semi-absentee parenting looked like from the kid's side, and it wasn't acceptable. I'd developed the discernment to anticipate what was likely to happen in the future and to order my priorities in the present around that. On the road, driving from Louisiana to North Carolina (again) and missing my son's first football game, I realized where my most probable future was headed. "Well, shit," I remember saying out loud to whoever's listening when you see Truth. "That's not going to work." It was against my core values. I immediately started running through scenarios of how we could build the business in alignment with what mattered most to me.

As a result of that revelation, AdvantaClean committed to the franchise path, and over the next three years, we sold all our company locations around the Southeast under a franchise model. At the time, it felt like burning the boats and heading into the jungle, but that was the course aligned with my values, so that's what we did. And it worked out okay.

VALUES ARE EXCLUSIONARY

In decision-making, your values form the first filtering pass of all possible actions and outcomes. You screen all your options through your values to exclude the unacceptable. It's the step that asks, "What are the deal breakers?"

Our true values delineate what we'll tolerate and what we won't. Being unwilling to travel constantly between the Gulf Coast, home, and our offices in Charlotte and Orlando excluded a lot of my options. Your values tell you what's in and who's out. They create your floor and your ceiling.

> Your core values are the first filter of your discernment.

VALUES ARE VISUAL

Your values are what you must have and what you will not

tolerate. If you tell me you value hard work but I see you slacking off, I know you value ease over effort. Integrity means walking your talk, but you'll do both in circles if you don't know what you truly value. Your values are observable. You can see what you value by looking at how you live. Take a look at what you do with your time and money. If you spend hours reading and many dollars on books or other kinds of training, you can be pretty sure you value learning.

If you don't like what you see, you have to get deliberate. Here, it can help to come at your values from the other direction, from aspiration instead of observation. What kind of person do you want to be? Bring your actions into alignment with your ideals. If you aren't maniacally conscientious about running your decisions through your values filter, you're going to make the easy choice instead of the right one.

The flip side is true too. The decision I made in the car that night was massive, life-changing, and the right one. I was able to make it pretty easily because I'd already done the work of figuring out what I valued. If you're clear about your values and you make a decision that passes only that first gate, you can't go too wrong. You may not make the best decision, but you'll make a better one.

Do this values-defining work for yourself, but do it with every group you lead. Step up and make this conversation happen. Not only will it get the rules and expectations right out there where everyone can see them so there's no disagreement about what's acceptable and what's not, but it's also a great way to build strong relationships too. Good agreements up front head off bad disagreements down the road.

Even when I coached young kids, I'd get everyone together to create this kind of agreement. Once we had our values spelled out, we were clear about how we did things, and we became the people who did things that way—instant tribe. I let the kids do a lot of the values-defining themselves, and we wrote down our Must Haves and the Won't Tolerates. Everyone knew how we were going to make decisions, and it took big swaths of behavior possibilities off the table from the start. It wasn't anything super complex—these kids were twelve, for God's sake—but we set out player rules, coaching commitments, and parent expectations. And we had a short list of values under each. Everyone knew what was expected from parents, what my commitments were to the team, and what the players could and couldn't do.

> Your values are what you must have and what you will not tolerate.

VALUES ARE VIRTUOUS

Because they're going to guide everything you do, your

values have to be things you really believe in and are willing to stake your name and even your life on. You must be willing to fight for them, to lose money because of them, and to filter all your decisions through them. When you catch yourself doing something that's not in alignment with your values, you stop and do something different.

The values of every team on which you play should be aligned with your own. In a bit, I'll talk about my personal values and my company's, but yours should be unique to you. Every family, company, team, or group needs values tailored specifically to it. What you value drives what you do, and what you do determines your opportunities. Values generate momentum. I want to help people be successful, but if someone's values aren't aligned with mine, then we're not playing the same game. If I want to help this guy and he wants to take advantage of me, it's not going to work.

> **MY VALUES**
>
> I value stewardship and grace. I value courage, grit, and humility. I earn my equity and invest in my reputation. I hold myself and others accountable. I work to always do more than is required or expected and to leave a legacy.

TESTS FOR VIRTUE

I know two great tests to make sure your values are virtuous: the Poster Test and the Pain Test.

The Poster Test means you're willing to put your values on your wall. If you live your life by rules you're willing to put on a poster for everyone to see, it's going to be hard for you not to do the right things. If you follow rules you won't post or post rules you don't follow, you can't be a business athlete. You can pick up a soccer ball, run it down the field, and throw it in the net, but you're not playing soccer. The business athlete's game has rules too.

Values have value—actual cash value—and they can be expensive. If yours are costing you money, it's a great (if unpleasant) sign that they're virtuous. They pass the Pain Test. I've lost more money than I care to contemplate because I wouldn't massage the facts to get out of paying a bill. I've walked away from opportunities and left money on the table. It hurt, but I never agonized over the decision. If something is against my values, I don't do it. I don't have to think about it. And here's the thing: being true to your values, while costly in the short run, will end up generating more profits, financial and personal, than you'd gain by sacrificing your integrity.

Recently, my wife, my 15-year-old son, and I went out for dinner, and when the bill came, I noticed we hadn't been charged for my wife's glass of wine. A different server had taken the order and likely overlooked adding it to the ticket. When I noted this aloud to my wife, I could feel my son watching to see what I'd do. It hadn't been an inexpensive glass of wine, but I suspect he already knew. I brought the error to the server's attention and reminded my son that "if you know what the right thing to do is, do that." It's a standard expression of mine, but I also believe not paying for the wine would have run counter to one of our explicitly stated Dudan family values: "Respect others." Knowing what you stand for and what you will not tolerate makes such decisions easy.

THE DUDAN FAMILY VALUES

Live fun.

Be humble.

Respect others.

Stay on purpose.

Never ever panic.

Be a servant leader.

Fail fast and push forward.

Trust yourself to take chances.

Always do more than is expected.

VALUES BUILD EQUITY

One of the best ways to make sure you're living in accordance with your values is to track them on a balance sheet. I'll give you some suggestions, but first I want you to think about this on your own. What are your assets and liabilities? Ultimately, your assets are the things you create, and your liabilities are the things you consume. Reading creates knowledge, and knowledge is a value. Watching TV consumes time. If you boil down your primary identity and your truest priorities, what moves you closer to who you want to be and toward what you value? What moves you farther away?

If you're having trouble coming up with your own assets and liabilities, think about a contrasting model. If you were going to write up a balance sheet for being a rock star, what would contribute to that identity and value set? Wild nights of drinking and maybe a drug arrest?

A balance sheet is a reconciliation of your assets and your liabilities, and your assets minus your liabilities equals your equity. Both assets and liabilities compound. Eat too much today, and it's going to be harder to exercise tomorrow. Yesterday's liabilities carry over into today. Conversely, make some deposits into the relationship account you share with your spouse today, and I guarantee tomorrow will go better for you.

Start with the kind of equity you're trying to build. I'll give you a hint: you want to build equity in the things you value. I'll give you a recommendation too. I see five areas where investing in your values can build personal equity: your relationships, your reputation, your health, your wellness, and your finances. Start with your relationships.

If you're a programmer, you might invest less in relationships than you would if you're in sales, but when you're hanging off a cliff by a fraying tree root, you're still going to want people who are willing to throw you a rope. The people who will do that, and then tie the rope around their own waists to save you, are going to be the people you've invested in. You've given them your time and shown them grace. They're the people you treated well when you didn't have to and the people you stayed fully present for when you were with them.

RELATIONSHIP EQUITY

When you've invested in a relationship with someone, when you've put in the time and the patience, when you've invested in grace and forgiveness, when you've lived your values with and for them, you have equity. (At least assuming you didn't make all those investments two days a year and were a total ass the rest of the time.) Value and invest in the right kinds of people. Spend your entire life searching for that handful of people you can really trust. Investing in selfish, cruel, lazy, or dishonest people is like investing paper money in fire. The flames will take everything you care to feed them and give back nothing but ash.

Figure out what really adds value to the lives of the people closest to you. When I sold AdvantaClean, I gave my wife a diamond ring because I wanted to honor her with a symbol that recognized that this journey would not have been possible without her support, her hard work, and her tireless attention to our family while the business of building a business went forward. It was a gift carefully chosen to be meaningful to her. If she didn't like jewelry, I would have done something else.

Investing your time and attention in the symbolic and practical things that are valued by the most important people in your life is an excellent practice, but you can build equity in your relationship with anyone by simply showing up with a good attitude. Being interested in people is an investment in them. Unsolicited compliments may be the absolute best investment in terms of how little they cost to give and how much happiness they create. They're free to you and gold to people. Give them often.

Build equity not just in your personal relationships but in your professional ones as well. People come to franchising to solve a problem. For some it's retirement; for others it's their kids' college tuition. Some are simply looking for a career that's less restrictive and more secure than working for someone else. No matter what brings them to business ownership, it's a full-contact, demanding, and stressful enterprise that comes with a healthy level of friction between franchisee and franchisor.

Here, too, alignment of values is critical. In prospective franchisees, I want to see at least these crucial three traits:

- Grit. I want to know they will commit, follow through, and persevere when things get tough.
- Intellectual humility. I look for smart people who aspire to learn, who will share their own knowledge respectfully, and who are willing to follow the plan with no attacks of "genius" for at least the first twelve months.
- Diplomacy. I need people who can skillfully resolve conflicts in a healthy way.

Building relationships is critical if you want to move at the speed of trust—a phrase taken from a great book by the same name. Even with a great plan in place, with a company's worth of people, and in a dynamic marketplace, something will inevitably go wrong. People sue against a contract. People sue companies. People rarely sue their friends. Having relationship equity with the people you're in business with means you'll probably get the chance to explain yourself and the opportunity to make it right for everybody.

Trust creates velocity. Doing business with people who trust you and whom you trust is frictionless. You don't have to constantly watch everything and everyone to make sure they're doing what they said they would, and you don't have to stop your own work to tie down every loose thread with a lawyer's knot.

I'm not saying do million-dollar deals on a handshake

(although I have), but especially within the organizations you lead, trust is absolutely critical. It's how you win your people's investment in your leadership, and it's the only way to know what to expect from them in return. I could never have made the decision to go on *Undercover Boss* if I hadn't trusted everyone in the organization.

I've had to make some very hard decisions about the future of my company. I've taken some very big risks that paid out big rewards. My ability to make those big bets rested on a bedrock of the trust I'd built.

REPUTATION EQUITY

Next, invest in your reputation. Your name will travel farther than you ever will. Your reputation is the relationship you have with people you haven't met, and creating equity here is about making contributions to your different communities.

In your business community or industry, step up, show up, and volunteer. This could look like anything from mentoring others to volunteering to speak or participate on panels. Let your words and actions prove your values in this arena, and your professional reputation will take care of itself. Be kind. Be thoughtful. Be charitable, capable, and effective. And for every conversation, be present.

Show up in the wider community as well—at your kids'

school, at town events, at fundraisers for local causes or charities, or hey, coach a team! Successful business leaders and many other people you'd like to meet understand the value of giving back, and contributing to the community can contribute to your professional network as well.

In both your professional and local communities, for every club, association, or organization you join, follow this rule of three:

- Show up for every meeting (most people show up once or twice, then ghost).
- Join a committee.
- Sponsor an event.

If something is worth the time to join, go ahead and fully commit.

If you show up, you'll gain a reputation for being present. If you treat people fairly, you'll gain a reputation for fairness. If you cheat somebody—even someone you'll never see again—you've still subtracted from your reputation's equity. Your ability to attract high-quality people as friends and employees is a direct function of your reputation. Having a reputation as the kind of person great people want to know improves the quality of your friendships and your future. The same thing is true of your business. Having a reputation as a great place to work attracts high-performing employees, and no organization is ever going to be any better than its weakest member. Reputation equity is money in the bank of your future success.

I once coached with a great linebackers' instructor who said football was all about angles and leverage. There are business athletes who play the same way. Most of us are either "angles and leverage" players or "respect and resolution" ones. I default to the latter. I'd rather work toward a resolution than force one, but some situations in business require you to maintain your angles and keep your leverage. Just remember that the balance of power changes all the time, and someone over whom you have leverage today may have the leverage tomorrow. In the absence of relationship equity forged from resolution and respect, you can expect that leverage to be wielded against you.

On occasion, while building AdvantaClean, we made some mistakes that caused everyone some pain. All companies do from time to time. It happens. But the relationship equity we'd built with our incredible franchise partners by adhering to our values of resolution and respect always allowed us to work together to find common ground and keep moving forward.

When I've made the decision to see a hard time through rather than to pull back and take a more cautious position, it's because I've looked at the organization I've built and asked myself: "What is the probability that we, as a group, will be willing to put in the work to see this through?" The only reason I could accurately make that assessment was that I knew what to expect from my people. I knew they trusted me, and I trusted them. So we went for it every time, together.

HEALTH EQUITY

Good health is like oxygen; you don't appreciate it until you try doing without. You cannot lead or help the people around you if you are in poor health, but this is not a health and fitness book, so this section will be brief and direct.

Invest your time, energy, and money to maintain good health. Build equity in the assets of sleep, fitness, and nutrition. Reduce the liabilities of processed food, drugs, and alcohol.*

*ON ALCOHOL

First, I am no one to talk. I have struggled with alcohol since the age of fifteen. Nearly all of my worst decisions and my greatest personal regrets are a direct result of my relationship with alcohol. They still haunt me. I am the least perfect person I know and no saint for sure, but I've come to believe that alcohol directly attacks the two most precious things in life: time and love.

Many of the people I've known who drank excessively simply stopped developing because they lost so much time to being drunk or hungover. In the hours you spend in either condition, you're not reading and contemplating the material, you're not having rich conversations, you're not making the music. It's putting in that extra 10 percent and doing more than is expected that lifts the extraordinary above the mediocre. If you're spending your free time drinking, you don't have it available to do the things that make the difference. Unless being drunk or hungover is your objective, being drunk or hungover takes you away from your objective.

Progress is made in the downtime, when others are resting. When the task has been completed or there's a lull in production, the flow of time ebbs and you can shift from the urgent to the important. These are the spaces in which to move some critical project ahead, realign your team, or solve a big problem. The music is made between the notes. This is why the wildly successful outliers are so few: most people aren't willing to rush into the void with purpose and emerge from a lull with a new beginning, strategy, understanding, and inspiration. You can work on yourself when you're off the clock.

Or you can just go get shit-faced. Your call.

I believe wellness habits are paramount to the accumulation of wisdom and discernment, but our minds are constantly under attack. Clarity and mental acuity are increasingly difficult to maintain. The screens are everywhere—on the wall, on our phones, on our wrists, even in our cars. We cannot live a normal life and avoid these inputs. These screens are an important part of the fabric of our society and the newest way we engage with it.

Put succinctly, feed your mind, your body, and your spirit with information and inspiration. If you want to dig deeper, I slice it this way:

- Train your mind.
  - Establish daily rituals.
  - Meditate.
  - Practice focusing versus multitasking.
  - Use a calendar rather than a to-do list.
- Feed your mind.
  - Eating the right food matters.
  - Protect your inputs: limit bad content, and input inspirational or educational content.
- Exercise your mind.
  - Read, debate, converse, think, strategize.

FINANCIAL EQUITY

On the hierarchy of entrepreneurial value creation, the top 10 percent of people are the innovators, founders, and creators of value. If you want to be in the top 10 percent, default to activities that create value. Take an inventory of how you spend your time and evaluate it by whether you're creating or consuming. What does playing games on your phone create? We all need ways to unwind, but look for things that are relaxing and still create value. Reading and even watching quality TV (or crappy TV with quality people) can create value, or at least not burn it for fuel. Additionally, find ways to create value while you're doing value-neutral tasks. Going from one floor to the next neither creates nor consumes anything, but if you take the stairs instead of the elevator, you've contributed a tiny bit to your health equity.

I've been around a lot of high performers, and they all seem to operate on the Create, Don't Consume principle. In fact, I've noticed an almost one-to-one relationship between people's level of performance and the percentage of work they do on their asset side. The highest performers throw a brick through their damn TVs and have other people dealing with their emails and schedules. They do a great job of delegating everything, they're constantly working, and they're brilliant. They don't do anything that doesn't leverage their core strengths to drive their equity. To them, doing any work that is not aligned with their core competencies or strengths is a liability, slows them down, and takes time away from their highest-yield activities.

It can get a bit neurotic, and it's a hard way to live, but they're so bought in to building their equities that it's what they do. I'm more balanced. I cherish my family time, and I've found that the older I get, the narrower my vision is about who I want to be and how I'm going to go about it. My discernment has honed my list of equity-creating activities to a well-defined edge. I make choices about what matters most and invest my time, energy, and focus there—work, family, faith. However I roll, I roll all in.

Little kids will play a different sport each season with maybe some dance or violin lessons thrown in, but by the time they reach high school, they've usually narrowed it down to fewer than three activities. The same thing is true of the business athlete. When I was younger, I spent a lot of time adding to the number of core competencies I had. I eagerly acquired tools to put in my business athlete's tool kit. Now I have my favorite four or five that I like best and know, and by dint of years of practice, I can wield them with mastery.

We all have to choose what the right portfolio of assets looks like for us based on what we're building it for. Based on who you want to become, based on your purpose and your vision, figure out what matters most and which activities go on what side of the balance sheet. Invest your time and energy in those which build the most equity in the most important areas, whatever those are.

Your values are always the first gate any decision has to clear. Once you filter out the options that run counter to your values, evaluate what's still on the table and what equity it will create. A red wine and steak night isn't against my values, but it will make a withdrawal on my health ledger. Deposits in the relationship column may well balance out those losses, and an extra half hour on the treadmill might zero them out. But a night of Cheetos and TV on the sofa *is* against my values, so I don't even have to do the math.

STRONG VALUES HAVE INTEGRITY

Your values are the first filter you use to sieve out options that are unethical or against your core principles. You then assess what's left and use it to build the most equity in the most important sections of your balance sheet, but there's one final exercise you need to add to the core-strengthening part of your discernment-building regimen.

We all believe that we're generally right. We look at the world through our own personal lens and believe our set of constructs is true. Nothing's wrong with that. You can and should believe in what you think is true. But if your individual values and personality goggles are the only ones you can see through when you're trying to weigh your options, you're going to miss some relevant data.

You build a business to get more done than you can do on your own and to divvy up the work. This delegating of responsibilities and tasks is a skill, and most people understand how important it is. Diversity of thinking and perspective is also valuable. Diversity is critical for the efficient development of our society, our businesses, and everything else of value. So when you build a business to accomplish a specific set of things and assemble a group of people to get those things done, you want to have diversity in almost everything—gender, race, age, skill, talent, and background—but not values.

Your company's values should be consistent with your personal values, but they don't have to be the same or even have much overlap. I personally value things that aren't on AdvantaClean's values list. And here's a paradox for you: I value diversity, but I won't tolerate diversity of values in my company. Everyone who works for me is welcome to believe whatever they want to when they're not at work, but when they represent the company, they must live its values. They are the ties that bind us together.

STRONG COMPANY VALUES

A company's values drive delivery on its brand promise. A

business is an outcome-driven organization, and its values must be tied to the outcomes it produces and the people it's set up to serve. At AdvantaClean, it was very important to me that everyone in the organization always kept in mind that we were the company people called on the worst day of their lives.

On the day a new customer first contacts us, their home—their biggest financial investment and the place they raised their kids—might have sewage backed up eight inches deep. Or its roof is gone. They've lost all the family photos. They still haven't found the dog. Our values had to be aligned with being of service to people in that kind of situation. We had to be what our customers needed: competent, respectful, and there to serve them. It was our mission to honor the opportunity, to know the right things to do, and to then do those right things to the best of our ability.

To take a counter-example, Zappos lists creating "fun and a little weirdness" as one of its values. I'm hardly anti-fun—in fact, "Live fun" is on my family's values list—but "a little weirdness" has no place in my company's values because of the kind of business we do. Zappos sells fun products. Their customers like associating themselves with good times and crazy chili cook-offs. The people we serve, in the times we're interacting with them, don't put a high premium on fun. AdvantaClean's values are tailored to its value proposition. They reflect what the people who need us need most.

A company's values drive delivery on its brand promise.

Personal values reflect and determine who a person is, and a company's values do the same. Additionally, they determine who can join the team and who moves up (or down) the ranks. If a company says it values accountability, but there's no penalty when its people don't do what they promise, accountability isn't really a value. On the other hand, if you've chosen your company's values well, they're important enough to its success that you won't be able to tolerate employees who don't adhere to them. Nobody likes to fire people, but I never had much trouble doing it because everyone knew what our values were and what wouldn't be tolerated.

And we hired on the basis of our values. We always shared our company values in the first interview any prospective new employee had, and I'd ask which value resonated most with them and why. You can learn a lot about a person by the way they answer both of those questions. If two otherwise comparable candidates both pick "respect" from the list, but one tells you a moving story about her grandfather, and the other shrugs and says respect just seems like a pretty good idea, it's not hard to decide who to hire. And you will have learned something cool about your new employee's family to boot.

You've learned something and you've taught something. By starting a job interview with a question about values, you demonstrate through action how important your company values are. I always started with values, then I'd tell people about the culture and the mission—what our people were like and what we were trying to accomplish. When I felt like the person I was interviewing would contribute to our mission, get along with our culture, and follow our values, I'd go back to values from the other side and tell them what we, as an organization, had of value to offer them. It was a great way of making sure people were going to be a good fit for the company before we brought them on board.

Not only did AdvantaClean hire on values, we franchised on them as well. As the final step in the approval process, we used to hold discovery days. Every detail of those events was guided by and highlighted our values. The welcome goodie bags included a copy of a book I'd written called *Hey, Coach!*, which was nominally about sports and kids but was really all about values. I always wrote a personalized note to each prospective franchisee and included a letter from the president.

We'd take them out to a nice dinner and head back to the hotel early. The next morning, I'd address the entire group and also talk to people individually. I'd use subtle ways of measuring them against our values, keeping a mental tally based on our conversations. Anyone who said they'd started reading *Hey, Coach!* got points. This wasn't my ego at work; it was a diagnostic tool. Reading meant they were readers, and people who read more are more successful. It also meant they were curious enough to pick up a book looking for insight into the company and the man who led it. That spoke to their level of preparedness and their work ethic.

I'd listen for what they had to say about the book to see if they'd been able to translate what I'd said about coaching to what we were doing as business leaders. If someone didn't get that it wasn't just a book about coaching kids, that told me something too.

I'd also ask the same questions I used with potential new hires. During my talk, I'd list our company values. While I was chatting with folks, I'd ask them which of the values resonated most with them. If they could articulate one and tell me a story about why, it was worth more points. "They all sound good to me!" earned none.

Finally, I'd ask people what brought them to the meeting in the first place. What was the most important thing they had come here to learn? Answers that demonstrated excitement, commitment, being part of our franchise family, and cultural fit showed that they had put in the work to understand the business, and they were just making sure this was the place for them. Answers that focused on how much money they could make, or on quibbles about lines in the contract that should have been answered over the phone ahead of time, deducted points.

THE POSTER TEST AT WORK

When you're working up the set of values that will go on your company's walls, the same rule about virtue obviously applies, but this list needs an additional feature: it needs to be punchy.

AdvantaClean put together the first iteration of our values statement around the time we started franchising to the public. It included everything we believed was important— eight to ten stated values followed by a little explanatory phrase. It was authentic and up on the wall, and we truly lived those values. We designed our training to be consistent with them, but we'd all have to check our memory against the poster. It was too wordy and too long to come rolling off your tongue like "bless you" after a sneeze. And that's what you want.

In 2016, I was on the road filming *Undercover Boss* for the longest I'd been away from home in years. There's a lot of downtime behind the scenes on a TV shoot, so I had time to think, and the experience gave me a new perspective (or a shift of perspective) on the company. I stepped back a little and saw it from a wider angle.

Within a month of getting back, I'd distilled our values down in response to what I'd seen and around what I believed was most important for us as a franchise network. I wanted something catchy and visual, so I came up with the acronym CARES: Community, Accountability, Respect, Excellence, Service. We bounced it around and pitched it to our franchise advisory council, and people loved it. We made posters and sent them to every location. We made CARES cards and gave them out in training. They got on everything we have. And I think it made a difference.

CORE VALUES

- **Community:** We make a difference in the community one person, family, friend, or neighbor at a time.
- **Accountability:** We do more than is expected by our own choice and of our own will.
- **Respect:** We treat others as we would like to be treated.
- **Excellence:** We set high standards and rise to them.
- **Service:** We meet others' needs with a servant's heart.

CHAPTER SUMMARY

Strong core values make the first decision-making cut. They exclude all non-acceptable options and delineate what you must have and will not tolerate. They must be based in virtue, build equity in those areas that matter most, and be internally consistent. Because they are so fundamental, they're well worth spending time to define clearly, both for your company and your personal life.

CHAPTER 3

PLAN YOUR GAME

SETTING DISCERNMENT-GUIDED DIRECTION

In the last chapter, I talked you through learning the game and setting rules about what you must have and won't tolerate, but there's another thing you need to know before you can start competing as a business athlete. Sports make the analogy painfully obvious. You can't play without goals.

Without a basket, there's no basketball. Football without an end zone is a bunch of big guys in tight pants smashing into each other. Without a home plate, baseball would be a ball, a bat, and walking in circles. Life and business are the same. Your values are your rules. You know you can't touch the soccer ball with your hands, but if there isn't a net at the end of the field, not only can you not win, you can't even play. You need a game plan that tells you where you're headed and how to get there. You have to define your destination and plan your path.

In high school, I had a couple of great basketball coaches who, looking back, were ahead of their time in the way they led us. They had an incredibly simple system—little cards they handed out to their players. The cards were numbered one through three and were called "goal cards." We each had one card for the entire season, where we'd write three season-long goals such as "I want to be a better left-hand dribbler" or "I want to be a better rebounder." Sometimes we'd do another card for an individual game and write in something like "get four rebounds" or "take two charges."

Coach encouraged us to make multiples of our season goal card and stick them up on our bathroom mirrors at home. Assuming you had decent hygiene (which *is* an assumption when you're talking about high school guys), your goal card would be one of the first things you saw every morning. He'd have us revisit our goals at regular intervals to see if we were on track or off and to recommit or adjust. To me, it was almost like magic. You could write down something you wanted to do, work toward it, and actually measure yourself against it. I've carried that simple exercise—taught to me at fifteen—with me ever since. It probably saved my life.

Some people are born with their success preordained and all their head-trash swept away by life, but that isn't true of most of the successful business athletes I know. Many entrepreneurs are screwed *into* existence. The rough starts and the hard falls drive us to swim ferociously just to get out of the currents we were born into. Circumstances force you to play the ball from where it lies, and play it again, and play it again. When you come from not much, risking it all to build a business doesn't feel like much of a gamble.

When I finally decided to put it all on the line and get going in life, I had that rudimentary goal-setting structure I'd gotten from basketball and a basic set of tools with which to make decisions that allowed me to get from where I was—if not all the way to where I wanted to go at first, at least moving forward.

DEFINE YOUR DESTINATION

Goals establish an immediate objective—get the ball in the net, cross the finish line, be a better rebounder, start your own business—and tell you where you want to go, but they don't tell you how you'll know when you get there. To set good goals, you need to know what winning looks like. Again, in sports, this is not terribly subtle. Winning means you've earned more points than the other guys. In business, you need to give it a bit more thought. To know what winning looks like for your company, you have to have a vision.

VISION

In 2004, I had complete control of an entire company for the first time. I had big goals for it, but high school basketball goal cards were the extent of the exposure I'd had to long-range planning and vision. The first investment I made was in my own education.

I hired a consultant who came in and put us through a six-month process that produced a seven-page vision statement. It spelled out what success would look like for AdvantaClean, and it guided our decision-making without an update until 2010. We had a vision of being ready, with the right teams and the right equipment in all the right places to respond quickly and effectively to the kind of emergencies that we were in business to help remediate. On the basis of that vision, we made a series of investments in trucks, equipment, and technology, and we put together a "rompin-stompin" disaster response team. Hurricane Katrina hit the next year, and preparation met opportunity.

Further, because that vision document established that we were going to become a franchise organization, we had the courage to execute on some huge decisions. We sold our flagship store in 2006 for seven figures. The next year, we sold another market, and in 2008, we sold our original location in Florida. When we sold all the stores, we kept only the commercial people. Everyone doing local business stayed with the location. We were only willing to keep selling the core of our business because we had a vision of what winning looked like, and it looked like franchising. I really had no perspective about how much it was going to cost to build a national franchise company, but I knew we had to be successful with our commercial services group to fund those plans.

By the mid-2000s, it was increasingly obvious that technology was just going to keep getting more central to every kind of business. I knew that if we committed adequate resources in time, attention, and financing, we could make technology a competitive advantage for us. Because we'd done the vision work, and because I knew franchising was our predetermined future and the best way to expand our business model, I hired a full-time tech guy. I gave him a mandate to make our technology so good that in a disaster situation, we could be executing while everyone else was still standing around trying to figure out what was going on.

> **Vision brings courage to discernment.**

Your vision tells you what winning looks like. It's a vivid and inspiring description of your destination. Your goals are the landmarks you know you need to hit on the way between where you are and where you want to be. It can help to think about this as an actual journey. Say you live in a small town in the middle of the country, and you have a vision of living in Paris. Because you can't fly from where you are to where you want to be directly, you know you need to get to a larger city first. Your goal, then, is Chicago. How you'll reach that goal—by plane, train, or automobile—is a strategy.

STRATEGY

For the first half of my career, I had no idea what "strategy" actually meant in business. For most people—certainly for me—goals and a killer work ethic driven by some sense of a better life are everything you need to be a successful person. That's fine, but to be a leader, you need a detailed vision and a solid strategy. Strategy creates clarity for everybody in an organization about what's important and what's expected. It converts your vision into something everyone can see, execute against, and measure. This is important because your people—even the very best ones—can't hear what you think.

I can prove it. Try this exercise: Pick a song in your head, and rap it out on the table with your knuckles as other people try to guess the song. I have done this in a hundred training sessions, and not one person has guessed right. The lesson: People can't hear what you think. We undercommunicate, then we hold people accountable for missing the mark when we failed to communicate clearly what was in our head.

This is what it's like to be a leader. My mind is constantly working three-part harmonies—past, present, and future—and I can see how they're all related. I'm working in tune with the melody one minute and an octave up the next, and nobody can follow that. It's confusing for people who chime in where I was sixty seconds ago. It creates discord. This is why, as a leader, you have to put in the time to break vision down into strategy and to communicate how all the different strands of that strategy come together. It's the only way people can align themselves with what you're seeing and match your pitch.

> **People can't hear what you think.**

Good leaders are emotionally contagious—able to transmit their vision, optimism, and dedication in ways that infect others with the same energy. They have enough command of themselves—of their facial expressions, tone of voice, and body language—to control how another person feels. This isn't magic, but the ability to be what I call "extraspective"—to see ourselves in the moment the way others see us. It's incredibly rare but, with practice, a trainable skill. Research shows that 55 percent of communication is nonverbal, and nobody's extraspective enough to convince people of what they don't believe themselves. People have a finely tuned phony filter, and—conmen and sociopaths aside—the easiest way to put that 55 percent of your communication to work advancing your agenda is to have no air between your words and your convictions. Authenticity matters.

Everything a leader does sends a message. The more coherent the message and the more it's being conveyed identically in the leader's words, actions, and subconscious expressions, the more power it has. Make sure the strategy you're communicating is in line with your values and advances your larger vision.

A lot of young entrepreneurs have a two-point strategy: get from Point A (make my next payroll) to Point B (what the company looks like when I die). I call this the Nickelback Strategy. You're scrimping and scrounging to get through next week, but hey, hey, one day you're gonna be a rock star.

Zero to Famous is not a strategy. It's barely even a daydream. Your goals tell you where you want to go. Strategy is what gets you there. It's the *How* to a goal's *What*. There are a lot of great books available on strategy. I highly recommend *Traction* by Gino Wickman. It's very simple and clean. You can also read *Good to Great*, and there's great stuff to be learned from *Mastering the Rockefeller Habits* as well. But at its simplest, strategy is closing the gap between where you are today and where you want to be at some point in the future, and identifying what steps will be taken to get there by whom, by when, and in what order.

You'll find a list of all my reading recommendations at the end of the book, but the basics of strategy are stone simple: Work backward from where you want to be to where you are now. Pick any flavor of strategy, make it part of what you do, and start doing. You'll know you have a strategy when you know what has to get done, who's going to do it, and by when.

Here's how to do it: Start by looking at what's possible in ten years and create a big, bold, inspiring vision. I spend most of my time on what Cameron Herold calls a "Three-Year Painted Picture" because the people I will be enlisting to help build it can wrap their heads around that time frame. Your job is to build a dream that is big enough that other people's dreams can fit inside it. Create your three-year goal with color and clarity so you know how your company will look, feel, and taste three years from now.

Next, ask yourself where things are going to have to be in one year in order to reach that Three-Year Painted Picture. Then, with your eyes on where you'll be in a year, set yourself a ninety-day mission. Ninety days is the ideal execution period—close enough to see, but distant enough to get meaningful things done. You should always be executing on a ninety-day mission.

PRIORITIES

Vision creates strategy, and strategy dictates goals and activities that lead to execution. Goals and activities need to be prioritized in order to deliver on strategy. Priorities tell you how to allocate your time, money, and attention. When AdvantaClean was still a small franchising company, we made a multimillion-dollar investment in our technology platform. It was a risky move—the single largest investment we made in a two-year period and for which we sacrificed a lot of profit—but it wasn't reckless. I made a vision-emboldened decision based on priorities that were based on a strategy that, in turn, was based on our goals.

We had a goal of growing AdvantaClean into a national franchise able to deliver information seamlessly with visibility, transparency, and continuity across the entire network of franchisees. That was my goal, and we weren't going to achieve it using the patchwork of software and systems that was typical in the industry. My goal led to a strategy of putting in place systems that would give us a competitive advantage. We were networked and sending out trucks while the other guys were still figuring out where theirs were parked.

That ambitious but clear and goal-based strategy set our priorities. More than maximizing profits, more than new offices, we were going to invest in what mattered most—an expensive technology platform, one we're still using today. It pays to put your money where your priority is.

> You have to water what you want to grow.

It's possible to keep breaking goals down into sub-goals to the point of absurdity. You take your ninety-day goal and break it down into monthly goals, break the monthly goals into weekly goals, weekly ones into daily ones, into hourly ones, into fifteen-minute increments. There are certainly people who work like that—people who know how each fifteen-minute phone call executes against their ninety-day mission—but most of the business owners I know work from a list. I think it's less important when I pick up the phone to know that the next fifteen minutes will move me closer to my goals than it is to track the impact path through each order of magnitude. In Chapter 8, we'll discuss the virtues of managing by a calendar over a task list, but lists are still a great way to order your priorities.

Every day, in the morning quiet—I wake up early just for the pre-dawn calm—I let my mind explore the dreams, visions, and future states that I have written into my future. I then drop back and check in mentally with the people in my life, the companies, the opportunities, and the strategies, and I test them for fit like puzzle pieces. I enjoy this type of dreaming—challenging myself to dream up a bigger future and then to identify what's missing and prioritize what's next for that day to create the most leverage and the greatest lift for all of it. I mentally touch base with my vision and ninety-day mission and use my discernment to make a decision about the three most important things I'm going to prioritize that day. This practice became an informal part of the culture at AdvantaClean. The Daily Top Three was never required, but it helped build a sense of unity. It was part of how we felt like a team with everyone contributing to the shared effort.

I used to love seeing those Daily Top Three emails come in each morning with everyone's list of the top priorities they wanted to accomplish with their workday. It was an interesting discernment litmus test too. You could almost spot the people who were going places by the way their lists weren't the same every day or just a laundry list of tiny nits they wanted to pick. The disciplined habit of prioritizing your day's work every day (with some bonus accountability if you're publishing it to a group) is the business athlete's version of rolling out of bed and doing burpees.

Having set your priorities by your goals and vision makes it easier to give each task your full attention. I believe strongly that one skill you must develop as a business athlete is the ability to focus your complete attention on something important and then to shift that attention on to the next thing and engage just as deeply. Shift and engage; don't juggle. Multitasking might make you feel like you're busy, important, and working hard, but sequential tasking gets things done.

PLAN YOUR PATH

When you're just starting to acquaint yourself with the ideas of values and strategies, goals, and vision, it can all start to feel very theoretical and confusing. It's not. The ideas are big and important, but executing on them doesn't have to be complicated. In fact, it shouldn't be. I've found two exercises—"Three Circles" and "Possible, Missing, Next"—to be incredibly useful in getting very pragmatic about acting on your vision and values and in planning a path toward the destination you've done the hard work of defining.

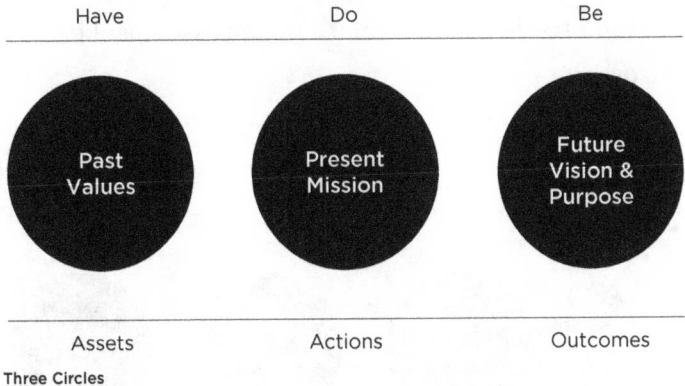

Three Circles

Get yourself a piece of paper and draw three circles like the ones here. In the far right-hand circle (future), write down your answers to the following questions: Who do you want to be? Who do your customers need you to be? Who do you want to be in the community? What does your business want? What do you stand for? What does your company stand for? What is your purpose for being? What does success look like? What other outcomes do you want?

Now move all the way to the far left. In this circle (past), list all your assets—everything you've collected over time. Include your financial assets, your social capital, your people, your values, your equipment. Now imagine that you lose all of those assets. At least once a year, put everything you have out on the curb and bring back in only those things that are aligned with your intentional future. I think of this part of the exercise as the Sacred Cow Killer. Knowing what you now know, would you reacquire the things you have and rehire the people? If not, get rid of the deadweight. Don't carry any part of your past forward by default. If you wouldn't re-choose it, then it's not an asset just because you own it.

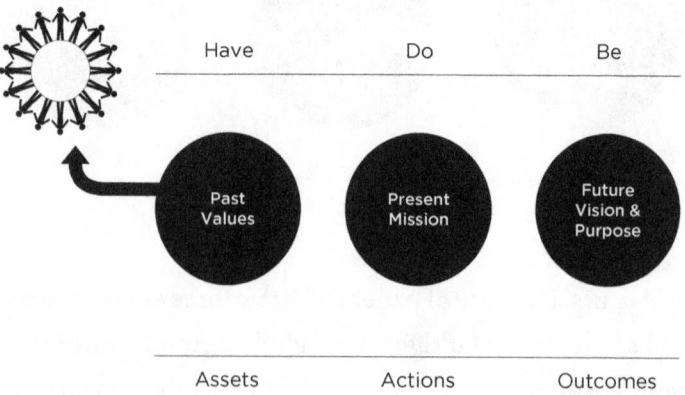

The center circle is where the work gets done. It's your ninety-day mission and your weekly goals. Think about what actions you're going to take to create the outcomes you want in the third circle. When you know where you want to be in the future and what assets you have—what you have learned, built, and accumulated in the past—you can live in the present, checking in regularly in both directions, future and past.

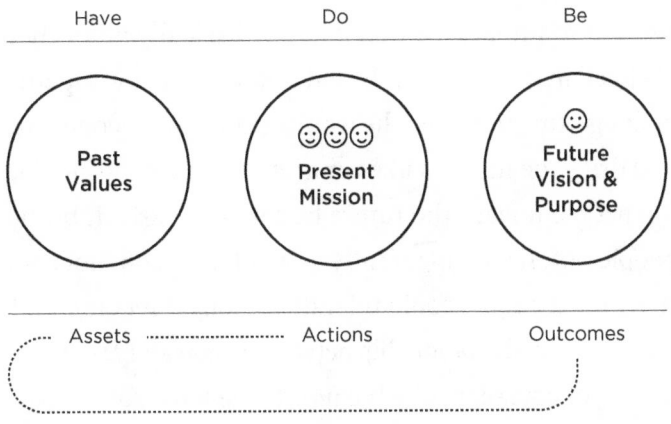

We've all known people who live their lives in the first circle, the past, but that's a fool's game. As a business leader, the center circle is where you want most of your people spending most of their time, but the third circle is where you need to concentrate your energy. You lead from this circle, but you must remember to communicate clearly back to the middle one. To be efficient in your present, you have to know your future. People can do their jobs efficiently in the present only if you've shown them where they're headed. It's your job to make sure there's a shared vision everyone is working toward, with shared outcomes and shared rewards.

> To be efficient in your present, you have to know your future.

Steve Jobs is an excellent example of an extreme version of this model. He was a true visionary who saw clearly what the future could be for the products and the industries he wanted to impact—which is to say basically all of them. He lived in that third circle and was so radically impatient about getting there that he would go into the second circle and drive the mission like a man on fire, pushing and kicking people toward the future he saw so clearly. It burned people out. It was apparently very fulfilling, but not something most people could tolerate for long. I recommend a more balanced relationship between vision and execution—unless, of course, you're the next Steve Jobs. You probably aren't. I'm certainly not.

POSSIBLE, MISSING, NEXT

Sometimes, to set really bold goals, you need to spend some time imagining what outrageous success would look like. It is your responsibility as a leader to create a bold future for the companies you lead. Nothing great happens until someone has the courage to make a bold statement. If your future could be anything, what would it be? Keep your answers to the realm of possibility—you're not going to get taller or younger—but otherwise, go crazy. It's possible you could make millions in the next year. It's possible for you to have more Instagram followers than The Rock. What is the most amazing set of accomplishments you can imagine? Expand your universe. Then engage your team.

Once you know what's possible, ask yourself what's missing. What isn't in place that would need to be there if you were already living everything you imagined? If you want more followers than The Rock but you don't have an Instagram account, that's something missing. As you work on the list of what's missing, you'll start to see new, more possible goals emerging. You'd put growing your Instagram followers tenfold in the next year on your What's Possible List.

Finally, ask yourself, "What's next?" Pick something from the What's Missing List and take action on it. Get yourself an Instagram account. Do it today.

THE PATH OF PROGRESS

This is a straight line.

When you think about moving from the second circle to the third—from your present to your future, from actions to outcomes—this is probably the path you imagine yourself taking.

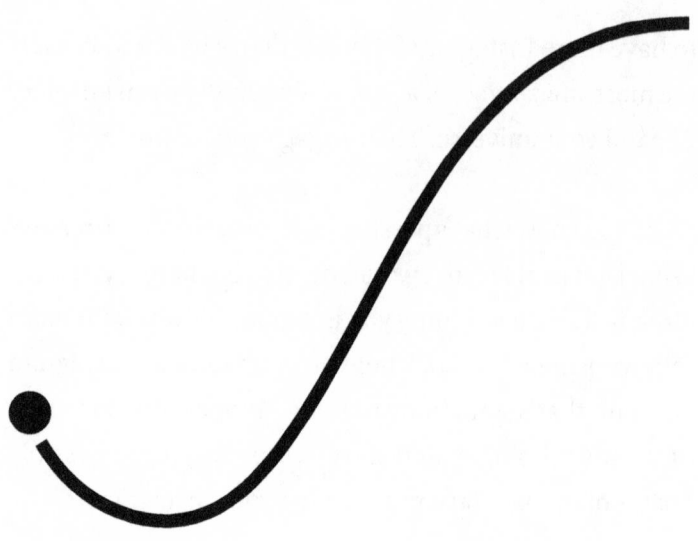

This is a Sigmoid Curve.

This is the way progress actually happens. The little dot is the present. It's right now. It's the place you begin when you undertake any worthy ambition.

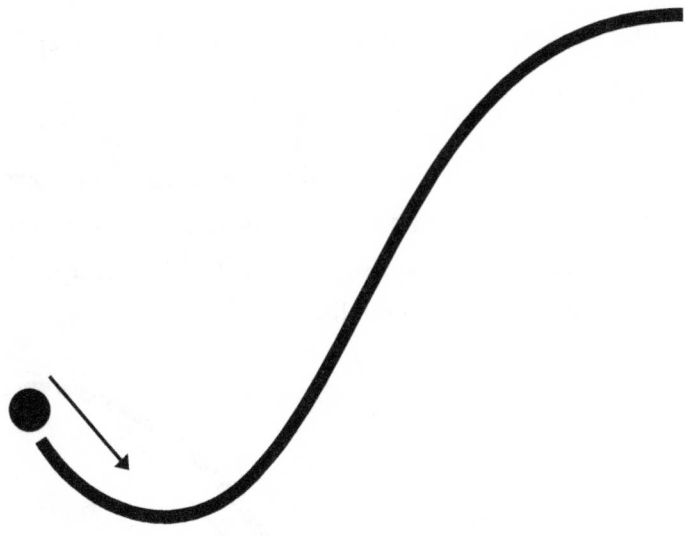

The first direction you go? Down.

Anytime you embark on anything, there's an initial investment—maybe in money, certainly in time and energy, often in risk or the fear of humiliation. Whether you've just agreed to give a speech or decided to open a new business, anytime you start something new, the first step isn't forward (or backward) but down. Say you're going to open a franchise. The first step is paying a franchise fee, getting certifications, and putting money down on a location. You have to put (an often scary amount of) money down, and you need to invest time and energy into training, all before you open the doors on the first day. Nothing good comes easy, but if you know to expect that downward dip at the beginning, you're less likely to get frustrated or discouraged. Don't think it means you're failing. The first step is always down.

If you stick it out, over time, things get better. You start climbing that hill. Your business grows, and you make back your initial investment and then some. It's all going up and up. But it's still not a straight line.

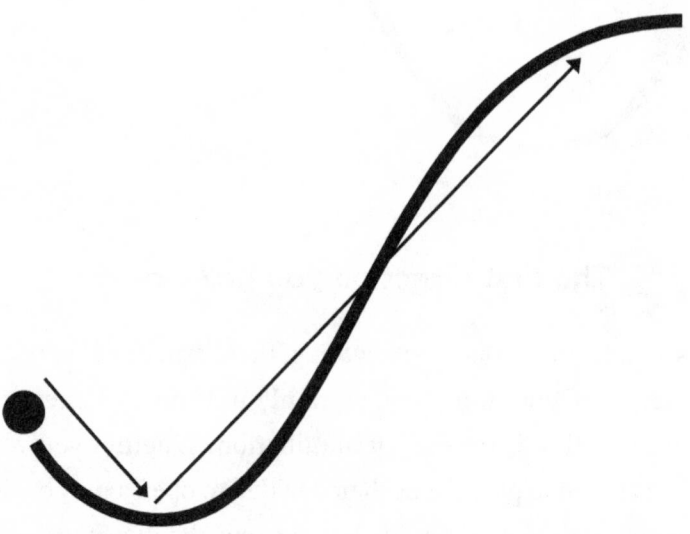

Every growth curve has constraints. Say you've opened an AdvantaClean franchise. You put in the time and money and have started to turn a profit and build a reputation, but there's only so much work you can do with one truck. You've reached capacity. You're at the top of the curve. You have more business than ability to deliver. You start to miss appointments, and you're paying too much in overtime.

You need another truck and more crew to meet the demand. You can only continue on any given upward trajectory for a limited amount of time until friction starts slowing you down, and the line starts to fall.

Without intervention, you'll keep dropping down into entropy. You've burned through the rocket fuel that got you through liftoff, and there is no booster rocket. You can't just buy a truck and hire some guys. The processes you have in place, which worked well for a three-person company, won't scale. As companies (and people) grow, processes have to be broken down and reorganized around the new normal. You have to re-launch. You're back at the point of embarkation, taking off, which means heading down again, possibly making additional investments in your business. You have to bend your knees before you jump.

You start a company with a scrum of three or four people, and everyone's in it together. But that doesn't scale. When an organization goes from four to twelve, it can't help but be less personal for each person. Now you need job descriptions and rules. You've gone from a loyalty organization to a performance organization. It's not bad, but it's different, and if you don't manage it differently, bad things can happen. And this dynamic never stops. I know a guy who built a $30 million business into a $500 million organization, and he said every time the company reached the next

$100 million in sales, he had to take the whole thing apart and rebuild it.

This is why a leader has to operate from the third circle. Most people, if they think about the future at all, expect it to look like the past. They expect their current trajectory to continue in the same direction indefinitely. When they're at point 2, they expect point 3 to be the same relative to point 2 as point 2 was to point 1. A leader must have the vision to recognize point 2 not as the latest pinnacle of triumph, but as the crisis it is. This moment is a crisis, even if it doesn't look like one, because it's where things get stagnant. The status quo is not on the go. And a great leader never lets a crisis go to waste.

While your people are executing on a ninety-day mission, you need to be looking ahead, anticipating the future. The better your discernment, the more accurately you'll be able to perceive where you are on the sigmoid curve of growth and anticipate the direction it's likely to go next. Rather than waiting until line A starts to drop, while it's still rising, you'll be planning point B, making sure your company is prepared to take that initial step down to start a new sigmoid growth curve.

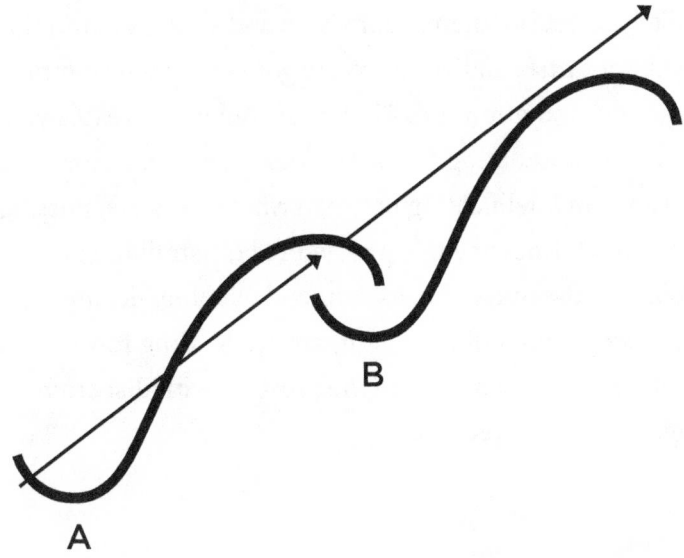

A

B

Before you have people executing on a ninety-day mission, before you're a leader, you still have to lead. When you're young, you practice leadership on yourself. Everything we've talked about up to now—learning the game, strengthening your core, and having a plan—applies to both company and personal leadership. In the next chapter, we'll diverge a little, but only a little.

CHAPTER SUMMARY

If you don't know where you're going, you'll never get there. To be efficient in the present, you have to know your future and clearly define the destination you're striving to reach. To do this, you need to have a clear vision and strategy for the future and to identify the goals and activities most likely to get you there. Your vision and strategy determine your priorities and where you're going to spend your time, money, and attention. That determination creates your path, triangulating between your values, mission, and vision, and delineating between what's possible, missing, and next. Knowing this path won't be a straight line; you plan for the initial dip, ascent, and eventual decline, and you stay ahead of the curve, always leading toward the future while managing in the present, with discernment guiding your direction.

CHAPTER 4

DRILL YOUR FUNDAMENTALS

DEVELOPING DISCERNMENT-BUILDING SKILLS

While the free throw is fundamental to basketball, it's fairly meaningless in soccer. For different sports and for different positions within the same sport, athletes drill on different fundamental skills. This isn't true for business athletes. Today, every business is a sales, marketing, data, and innovation business, and every business athlete is going to need a fundamental level of skill in those areas. When you're leading a team, you won't be down in the weeds using all of these skills every day, but you'll be managing people who do. Until you get there, self-leadership means learning and drilling on these fundamentals.

I got my first real job in seventh grade working as a busboy in a Chicago Mexican restaurant. By the time I was a freshman in high school, I had several thousand dollars in cash under my mattress and very little adult supervision. It went about as well as you'd expect.

At Schaumburg High I was primarily a basketball player until they brought in a new football coach who wanted to throw the ball. Who better to recruit to catch it than basketball players? I saw Coach Cerasani up on the shelf watching us scrimmage, and the next day he came to my biology class, took me into the hallway, and asked me to come out for the football team. That moment and the extra effort he took to have a conversation with me changed my life forever.

I graduated from high school with a GPA slightly above a 2.0, and when I showed up at the University of Northern Iowa, I was untrained in both academics and football. I had no fundamentals. I was just a kid trying to figure it out, looking for somewhere to belong, no idea where I was headed, looking for significance, progress—something. I ended up walking onto the football team, where I promptly had my behind handed to me. It was truly a baptism by fire. I hadn't had the years of training the other guys had, but I really liked the game and thought I could do well eventually. After one semester, though, it was clear no scholarship money was headed my way. I didn't have family money, and taking out more loans when I was dragging in a freaky freshman GPA of 1.9 seemed, let's say, less than wise. I didn't tell school or the team I was leaving, and I didn't call home. I just showed back up. Not coping, quitting.

It was a defining moment in my life. I'd gone away to play college football, I hadn't made the grade, and I was coming home. Life had not rewarded me for doing what I'd always done—partying and skating by. It was a very rough landing. When I got back, I realized very clearly that if something didn't change, I was never going to get out of there again.

So I changed.

To a kid who'd been working behind a bar until two in the morning at the age of twelve, the people I'd seen swanning off to college on their parents' nickel with their nice clothes, stable home lives, and entrenched study skills looked like assholes. I didn't want to be those guys—there was no way I could have been—and I took a kind of rebel pride in it. I didn't want to play by their system's rules, and I'd always figured I could just make up my own. I was smart and tough, and I could get things done. But the way I'd been doing things had stopped working and stopped hard, like hitting a tree.

If I wanted a better life and I didn't want to use *their* system, I needed to make a better one and figure it all out myself. What were the things I needed to do? How did I need to be smarter? Where did I need to get tougher? What did I need to do to win? I'd had some wins on the athletic field, and I thought maybe the goal-setting that my coaches had taught me could translate to the rest of my life. It was the only option I could see, so I put that philosophy into practice and tried to make my system work.

From where I was standing, I could see just one path out, and it looked like athletics and college. My Grandpa Leo told me flat out that I was not fast enough to play college football. Ouch. But I'd heard the same from college recruiters, and I knew it was the truth. I didn't like hearing it, but I loved him for saying it. I had decent agility and quickness (probably a result of my basketball training), but my straight-line speed was a nonstarter (probably a result of my bowed legs and lack of flexibility). I needed to be faster if I wanted a scholarship, so I set about trying to solve that problem. I enrolled in a local Taekwondo academy and hung a heavy bag up in the garage.

At the Chicagoland version of Last Chance U, William Rainey Harper Junior College, I joined the football team. The school was a football factory where every starting sophomore typically moved on to a Division 1 program. We were a mob—players who needed some academic, athletic, and/or behavioral...let's say "refinement." Most of all, we were talented players who needed a chance. This program gave us one, and we won nearly all of our games and competed for what amounted to the JUCO National Championship on the regular. The crowds were small, we bought our own shoes, and we played Saturday mornings. It was a lot of fun.

Whenever I wasn't at school, I was in the garage working out. My old friends would come by to grab me and go have some fun, but I stayed head down. I focused on school, I focused on athletics, and I kept myself straight. I went from being a person who only did the things he wanted to—partying, drinking, and playing sports—to somebody who tried to do everything well, no matter what it was. Two years later, I was offered a full scholarship to a number of colleges, including Rice University, and I ultimately selected Appalachian State.

This is the mentality of the business athlete. You figure out what you need to do to get where you want to go (and if that sounds familiar, it's because it was the whole last chapter), and then you get after it. You don't need to pick up a martial art to be a business athlete (although it can't hurt), but you do need to get faster. In football, the equation for speed is flexibility plus strength plus explosiveness. In business, it's sales plus accounting plus HR plus marketing.

CEOs are like general contractors; they need expertise in every area of specialization that comprises their business, and they need to be the one with a plan. A good general contractor will have enough knowledge about plumbing to know whether the plumber is doing the job well or poorly, what that job should cost, and how long it should take. A general contractor also needs to know how to correctly sequence different aspects of the overall project so that the HVAC crew doesn't show up to run ducts before the house is framed in.

Great entrepreneurs can usually do every job in the company they run if they need to, but they don't. They do only the highest-value work where they can deliver the most impact. You won't have the discernment to know what that work is unless you know what's involved in performing all the tasks that need to be done. You must build that knowledge base early in your career so that later, you'll know what you shouldn't be putting your time into. For the most part, that means handing off the jobs at which you are most proficient because you'll be best able to discern if others are doing them correctly.

SALES

As soon as you can afford to (if not before), invest in sales training. It's expensive, but that's because it's worth it. I got my training through Sandler, but I think the flavor you get is less important than getting it early and eating it up. I recommend just picking a program and getting started. There's absolutely no reason to postpone. Sales is a part of everything all of us do our entire lives. We sell ourselves to the people we'd like to date and marry. We sell our companies to prospective clients and employees.

Workers get paid an hourly wage, but business owners get paid by the conversation. Because your income-earning potential is directly tied to your ability to move a person from one position to another through conversation, it literally pays you to be incredibly intentional and thoughtful about how you conduct those interactions. Why try to figure out all the different processes and elements of that yourself when there are years of research and experimentation from which you can benefit? Surgeons don't cut without training. You have to practice and pass a test before you can drive. Your success depends on your ability to sell. Have the humility to learn something about how to improve your performance.

> Business owners get paid by the conversation.

There's not a person in the world who couldn't benefit from the ability to manage and organize conversations to successful outcomes. I don't care if you're dealing with prospective buyers, your children, your boss, or your friends; understanding how to shape a conversation toward a mutually beneficial outcome is going to serve you (and them) well. Even if you're not yet or no longer in an official sales position, you're still a buyer, and a better understanding of sales relationships and processes will help you make smarter purchases and pay less for them.

Nobody wants to be manipulated. We all like to think we make all of our own decisions based on rational consideration and without undue influence, even if we know it isn't entirely true. We're so allergic to the idea of being manipulated that we'll pull away anytime we feel the sales process in action. Conversely, if you're authentic and genuinely interested in other people, they can sense that and appreciate it.

I'm a very relational seller. I want to connect with people. For me, the bonding and rapport stage of sales is particularly important, and I work to establish trust and authenticity very quickly. Being a good relational seller requires two critical sub-skills: being palatable and being authentic.

Be Palatable

Palatability is more obvious in its absence than its presence. If you've just met someone and you can't wait to get away from him, or if you feel actively repelled by the guy, he hasn't made himself palatable. Palatability isn't the same as being charismatic or even likable—those traits are "you" focused. It's the ability to make the other person feel comfortable and engaged with. Mostly this comes down to nonverbal things. What do your expression and your body language convey? Are you relaxed and comfortable? Are you confident and unhurried? Do you feel to the other person like someone they already know, like, and trust? Do you make them feel like they're the most important thing in your life in that moment?

Be Authentic

People can spot a fake, so be real. You'll enjoy your life and your work a lot more if you can take a real interest in other people and genuinely engage with them. When you get this right, sales calls feel like you're just hanging out. You're looking for the feeling of "Man, we've been talking for five or ten minutes and having fun, but I guess at some point, we're just going to have to get down to business." When you build a real and personal connection with someone, they want to do business with you.

I tend to take this a step further than most. To me, that interpersonal piece really matters, so it isn't something I do just at the beginning of a conversation as a way in. I go back to it. I'll be doing business and something will come up, and I'll get right back into the personal stuff. The next thing you know, we're laughing, the guy's talking about his kids, and *he's* the one saying, "Okay, we've got to get this done." You want to build a relationship with people to the point where work feels like it's getting in the way of how much you're enjoying each other's company. That's when you've done your job. That's when it's time to be efficient, get professional, and go for the close.

DON'T JUST SMILE: "SMIZE"

Authentic smiles include the eyes. You can fake a smile, but you can't fake a smize.

THE SALES PROCESS

With a relationship in place, the process of closing a sale consists of insight, articulation, and authority. You need to be able to deeply understand your potential customers' problem, effectively articulate why you're the best solution to that problem, and have the authority to gently but firmly hold them accountable. Sales is a process with defined steps, but it should always feel organic and unscripted, even if you've planned it all out ahead of time. This requires you to be insightful, articulate, and authoritative.

Be Insightful

There are two component skills to being insightful: listening and locating. As part of developing a relationship with a potential client, you'll do a lot of talking. It's critical that you're also listening. Not hearing—listening. Real listening creates trust and fosters relationships, and it's also how you learn what your customers need.

While listening, learn to locate their points of pain. Find out where you can help. Maybe they have an old problem and a solution that isn't working as well as they'd like. Maybe they have a new problem and no solution. Maybe—and this is where the masters land gigs nobody knew were on the table—they have a problem they don't know about. Remember, in Chapter 1, I said that most people do things the way they've always been done. Often, this isn't the best way, but people put up with it because it's never occurred to them to wonder if there's a better way. Insight solves problems, even problems others don't see.

Be Articulate

You need to develop enough facility with language to clearly and compellingly articulate the most significant advantages your product has, not only over the competition's offerings but also over doing nothing. Sometimes it's obvious that you're better than using the next closest alternative, but you also have to be better than doing nothing at all. Great sales-people weaponize the insights they have into the potential client's pain points to articulate that difference in such a way that it simply doesn't make any sense to do nothing or to go with anyone else. You have to be able to express not just what's great about you, but what's great about you *for them*.

Be Authoritative

You should have expertise in your product, but anyone who

knows just a little bit more about something than somebody else can position themselves as an expert. You can
easily establish yourself as an authority on your product
or service, but if you don't also have the personal or moral
authority to hold people accountable, customers will take
everything you'll give them. They'll take your time educating them and running pricing scenarios, they'll take your
information, and then they'll give you the dreaded "I'll
think it over." Worse, they'll take it all from you and then
give their business to some cheaper, second-rate option.
This isn't because they aren't good people. I firmly believe
most folks you'll encounter in business are honest, decent,
and fair-minded. If you asked them to make a commitment,
they will live up to it. Too often, salespeople just don't ask.

I start making agreements with prospective clients very
early, and I remind them of those agreements and rein-
force them regularly. Usually, this comes in the form of the
question "If I could do X, would you do Y?" Good sellers
always create a clear future and get commitments on next
steps. Sales is a process, and good buyers appreciate a seller
who's efficient throughout.

In the question "If I could do X, would you do Y?" X could
be to lower the price by a certain amount, hit that dead-
line, deliver that capability. Y could be to sign the contract,
put down an advance, make a commitment. You can work
this kind of question into your information-gathering fairly

easily. These questions not only help you establish what's most important and what it's worth to the customer, but they also help protect you. Later, if they start to pull away, you can remind them that they've already made a commitment. I'll bet they'll honor it.

CHOOSE YOUR TRAINING WISELY

I said earlier that I think the method of sales training you get is less important than getting lots of it, but I'll caveat that with one piece of advice: expect one of the worst experiences you'll have in your business career to be buying sales training from a sales training organization.

Simply by virtue of the fact that they have to prove how good they are, they're going to be very difficult to negotiate with when it comes to price. They want your business, but they have to make it difficult for you because their sales pitch is also a demonstration. This is as it should be. Don't buy sales training from someone you can get the upper hand on in negotiating your purchase price for their training. (Same goes for hiring good salespeople—if they are too easy to close, how good are they really?) There aren't any new ideas in sales training, so you won't be missing out if you move on and find someone you can't beat.

FINANCE AND ACCOUNTING

Basic accounting is another fundamental skill every business athlete needs. If you don't understand what the elements of a balance sheet are, how to read a profit and loss statement, and how those things play into the health and value of your business, you can't measure performance. In order to be efficient in the present, you have to know your future. In the same vein, you can't make good business decisions without knowing what contributes to creating a better (or worse) balance sheet. It would be like playing a game for a year without keeping score, then looking at each other and asking, "Who do you think won?"

Not having a strong command of what you want your financials to look like at the end of a quarter and not knowing which levers to pull or what drivers will achieve those targets is like flying an airplane in the dark with no instruments. You can pick out a city by the density of lights. You can recognize a coastline. But what happens in heavy cloud cover or if you get out over the ocean? You'll have no way to know if you are getting low on gas. Your financials are the instruments that show you where you are and, on the most fundamental level, whether or not you're okay.

You don't have to enjoy it, but if you're going to be a business athlete, mastering the basics of accounting and finance have to be part of your regimen. You don't have to be an investment banker or even excellent at math; you just have to be good enough. Later, you can hire for excellence, but to get there, you need to have enough knowledge not to fly your company into the abyss.

WHERE TO LEARN YOUR NUMBERS

This is where your side hustle comes in. You have to actually *do* something to learn it. Start a business and use it to practice your skills. To get those skills in the first place, take classes. I think this is one place where you'll benefit from a live instructor. Find the courses you need online—you'll be able to go faster than you can at your local community college. This material doesn't need a Harvard professor to teach it, but it's not something you can learn as easily from a book, and nothing about it is intuitive. You might be able to figure out how to close a sale without training (you should get it anyway), but you absolutely won't be able to fake your way through your spreadsheets. Take Basic Accounting I and II and Basic Finance. Then call the trade association of whatever industry or industries you expect to go into and ask what other, specific kinds of accounting you'll need. Contractors, for example, should take cost accounting, and retailers need to know inventory account management.

HUMAN RESOURCES

We'll talk later about building a great company culture, but having a grasp on the basics of HR should be part of your training in the fundamentals. Your people deserve your consideration. You can't be the only person you're focused on. A man wrapped up in himself makes a very small package. Your entire organization will do better when your people do well, and the ability to attract, retain, educate, and manage people is crucial to your success. The well-being of the people on your watch is a huge responsibility.

I believe time is our only true currency, and if someone comes to work for me, that means they're giving me the most valuable thing they have. I take that very seriously. I'm not going to have people giving me their lives by the hour so I can own a yacht. I'm going to compensate them well, give them every opportunity to make the most of our time together, and make meaningful progress that contributes to their success. Then they can buy the yacht and invite me over.

Your two primary responsibilities to your people are to compensate them fairly and to create, if not actual progress, at least a vision of it. When a new employee joins your company, you want them to feel like a leaf coming to land in a stream, not a stagnant pond. If, from the first day, people feel like they're learning and growing and moving forward, they're going to produce smarter, bigger, faster results.

Your company may not always be moving forward, but when it isn't, it's your job as its leader to provide the business equivalent of those spools of painted scenery that old movies used to loop behind a stationary car when they needed a shot of someone driving. A good leader can (and does) create a sense of the company's progress. HR provides some of the tools that help you ensure your employees are making personal progress as well. People like feedback, and things like performance reviews and evaluations help them know how they're doing.

Beyond that, some basic training in HR best practices will create a safe working environment where people don't feel threatened or harassed and will keep you from running afoul of legal hiring practices and employment-related taxes. Most cities have employer associations, and they're a great place to start. They'll have resources on how to hire, attract, and retain people, guidelines on compensation, and information about taxes.

MARKETING

Marketing leads the way. There is no business without sales, and no sales without leads, so this is really the tip of the sword. It's the first point of contact between your company and the world of potential customers or clients. Good marketing articulates a set of promises about who you are as a company and what value you have to offer. It needs to communicate how you can help your customers and ideally initiate a dialogue in which both the company and the consumer reach an agreement that they're better together, each contributes to the other's greatness, and it's to their mutual benefit to exchange resources.

LEARN BEST PRACTICES

It's a good idea to read books on marketing to familiarize yourself with marketing terms, constructs, and best practices. Marketing involves many core skills you'll need in order to make sales. Marketing also involves clearly articulating the compelling advantage of your solution over the competition's and over the customer doing nothing.

CHAPTER SUMMARY

CEOs, like general contractors, typically have expertise in every area of their business, but they also have the discernment to know what *not* to do. With the exception of revenue, if any given area isn't a strength, you should delegate it. But business owners must stay close to revenue always. I've seen too many business owners be held hostage by their salespeople. If you want to lead your business, you need to take a position near the front of the house, and then hire and train the back of the house. In larger organizations, you are less exposed and can hire and retain talent on the sales side too, but I bet most CEOs get touches on their largest customers and most important relationships, no matter the size of the business. Beyond that, expand upon and live within your strengths. Hire for, delegate, and manage your weaknesses.

CHAPTER 5

TRAIN YOUR TALENT

GETTING DISCERNMENT INTO THE GAME

As a teenager, Lou Holtz was a scrawny linebacker with terrible eyesight. Today, he's in the College Football Hall of Fame. How'd he get there? He didn't have a growth spurt.

Lou knew he hadn't been born to play football, but he loved the game and wanted to be around it. He had no illusions that it was going to be easy to have a career in a sport he wasn't cut out to play, but he had the courage to try. He was an undersized linebacker at Kent State and after graduation decided to shift into coaching. With hard work he turned his passion for the game into a storied career in college football. When his career path as a player didn't work out, he found another way to stay in the game, and it paid off big. If you want to be a business athlete, you're going to need the same level of self-awareness, flexibility, grit, and humility to find and train your talent.

SELF-AWARENESS

Where do you think Lou would be now if he'd stubbornly committed himself to continuing his dream of being a pro linebacker? My guess is the decision would have been made for him. There *are* absolutes in life, and he absolutely would not have made the cut. Lou was determined. Moreover, he was flexible. When he took a realistic look at his talents, interests, and abilities, he recognized that his linebacker dreams played to his weaknesses. I doubt your professional aspirations are as potentially crippling as Lou's, but I encourage you to make the same kind of unflinching self-assessment.

WHAT'S YOUR PROFILE?

I recommend starting with any or several of the credible personality and skill profiling tools you can find online. I don't mean personality games like *Which Breed of Dog Are You?* I mean the real deal, such as Kolbe, DISC, Culture Index, TalentSolved, and Myers-Briggs.

These tests won't tell you everything you need to know about yourself. Context plays a role in personality testing because we tend to manifest different strengths or characteristics in different environments. It's easier to recognize a profile or trait in others than in yourself, so profile tests tend to work best when you take them as a part of a group. Tests like these can help you gain a keener awareness of your individual inclinations.

Personality profiles can be informative, but there's no substitute for simply putting in the hours in areas of study you love and find fascinating. You should take your passions and inclinations into account, and not discount them just because they don't show up in your personality assessment. For instance, I didn't stay up reading business books on the bathroom floor late into the night because a test told me to. I did it because I had an insatiable desire to learn business.

Everyone has a talent for work. Develop yours through discretionary effort. You can have your personality assessed and gain some important self-awareness that way, but your skills are going to have to be tested and proven in the real world. Success is never an accident. It's a habit.

Lou knew he wanted to live his life around football. If you're reading this book, I'm guessing you already know you want to win in business, but it might not be obvious yet which of your strengths to focus on. That's okay. Remember, discernment is a master trait of the business athlete, and nobody's born with it. Discernment relies on experience-based wisdom. As you put in the effort to discover and develop your talents, you'll be gaining that experience.

> Success is never an accident. It's a habit.

Most people have a natural inclination toward certain areas or kinds of work. Some people are happiest working with their hands, while other people have a knack for numbers. Assessments like the ones I mentioned earlier can help you zero in on your natural abilities.

For example, there are meta-traits associated with "generalists" as opposed to "individual contributors." IT people frequently align near the far end of the individual contributor profile, while CEOs are often generalists. Knowing where you fit along that continuum will help you identify and develop your strongest talents and traits.

Beyond the usual traits and skills that assessments can point out, there is another meta-trait, self-awareness, that is involved in thinking critically about yourself. Great business athletes develop the capacity to do this kind of self-assessing and learn to quickly self-correct. It's a characteristic I've noticed in many successful business leaders, and one I've come to deeply respect.

I've heard people who you'd think had nothing left to learn talk with great excitement about a new tool they acquired at a conference, a new perspective they picked up from a book, or an insight they gained from working with a coach. It's not just that they're learning new things; they are also integrating them. They are skilled at breaking concepts down to fundamental parts and reconstructing them in new ways. It's the basis of innovation.

Good leaders need to have that kind of introspection, the ability to look into their own inner workings, tally their strengths and weaknesses, self-assess, and self-correct. You need to develop not only a finely tuned awareness of your experience, but also of how you are experienced. What is it like for other people to be around you? It's a skill I was sorely lacking in my cuss word T-shirts and mullet. The best thing I can say about the way I presented myself back then was that it was open to change. And it did change, thank God.

FLEXIBILITY

Like Lou, I had NFL dreams. He aspired to be a linebacker; I had a vision of my future as a safety. (I never would have called it a vision, but that's what it was.) Also, like Lou, I was by no means an NFL-caliber player. I'd never played defense either, but I thought I'd have a better chance there than on offense. I assessed my strengths: I was quick, but I didn't have good straight-line speed, so improving that became a goal. I knew that speed had a lot to do with strength and flexibility. I was already working on increasing my strength, so I gave priority to increasing my flexibility. I didn't know how to do that at first, but I found that when you really prioritize a thing, it's top of mind enough that when possible solutions happen by, you're able to put the pieces together.

I don't remember how Taekwondo crossed my path, but when it did, I remember thinking, "Dang, those guys are flexible!" So I signed up. I was already doing everything my coaches told me to, but I assigned this to myself. I'm still not sure how I paid for it, but it improved my flexibility, which improved my speed just enough to earn me a scholarship offer from Appalachian State. My senior year there, we played against North Carolina State and Clemson with 77,000 people in the stands, and I started both those games in the backfield as a running back. It wasn't the NFL, but that audacious vision got me further in football than I would have gone otherwise. And it got me to college, where I set my sights on different but no less outsized business goals. To go fast and get far, your thinking has to be flexible too.

GRIT

If I were to design a business athlete from scratch, like some kind of entrepreneurial Frankenstein, the quality I'd build in first is grit. Grit is a muscle you can, and absolutely must, develop and train. I highly recommend Angela Duckworth's book *Grit* for a deep dive into the subject and tips on how to develop it in yourself. Anyone who sticks with anything long enough will ultimately have some modicum of success. The simple art of not giving up is one you must master.

For some people, reading and comprehension come easily. For others, they don't. Many people struggle with dyslexia or focus, while others have personal or physical obstacles to overcome. You might think it would be the people to whom everything seems to come easily who have the most success, but experience and history have taught me that's not the case. Often the people who have a steeper hill to climb get farther faster exactly because they have to work harder.

Life will show you what you're good at. It will show you where your particular talents and abilities lie, *but only if you're out there trying things*. You'll never discover you have super strength if you haven't tried lifting something heavy. You can't find out you have the ability to leap tall buildings in a single bound if you don't jump. You have to try things, and you have to pay attention. I didn't know I was a decent writer until a college English teacher singled out some of my work. I'd never thought of myself as being good at that kind of thing, although I'd read a lot. Your talents will be revealed to you if you're paying attention, and if you don't let other people's or your own head-crap get in the way. Figure out the things you're good at and develop them.

The first time I went out to Appalachian State, it was one of only three colleges I visited. There wasn't time to do more. I met with the coach, who had a name you couldn't help but love—Sparky Woods. His leading receiver had been a tight end who had retired early, so he needed somebody, and he took enough of an interest to fly back to Chicago with me and meet my dad. We went out to dinner, and Sparky said, "Look, pack the kid up in the car, send him out here, and we'll take care of everything."

It sounded great, but I didn't have a car. My mom had a 1972 Buick LeSabre that was dying a slow, rattling death. She let me have it, and I packed it with a couple of trash bags of everything I owned. I drove that car to North Carolina, parked it on a hill behind the university, grabbed my stuff, and took a shuttle down to the school. I was determined that going to college on scholarship would be a one-way trip. I never went back for the car.

I arrived on campus that day owning five T-shirts, only three of which didn't feature profanity, and with an ultra-mullet—long hair in back and the rest of my head shaved nearly bald. That was how I showed up for Accounting I, looking like an asshole criminal. Accounting was hard; I'd never had that kind of math and I'd barely managed a 2.5 GPA in high school, so the accounting professor had a lot of fun with me. We'd be discussing the Securities and Exchange Commission—the SEC—and he'd clarify, "Now Jeff, that doesn't mean the Southeastern Conference."

I still vividly remember his first test; I got 94 percent. He called me up after class to tell me it was one of the highest grades in the class. It was the first good grade I'd ever gotten in a legitimate college class (not the sixty-plus credit hours I had picked up in Olympic Weightlifting, CPR, and First Aid One through Five). College accounting—hell, college in general—was a gamble for a kid like me, but I wasn't scared to try things. Maybe when you've been knocked back hard with an obvious failure like I'd been, risking everything to really crush it at school and football doesn't feel so scary. That first A was enough to show me I had at least a little talent for business. I doubled down and developed it.

> If you're not living on the edge, you're just taking up space.

HUMILITY

The worst possible combination of traits is ignorance plus arrogance. We all know people who've taken this stance: "I don't know much, and I'm pretty sure I'm right about everything." They're some of the most obnoxious (and usually unsuccessful) people around. I can put up with an arrogant expert (although I prefer the simply confident one), and the humble idiot isn't hard to tolerate. But we're all ignorant about something, and without the humility to recognize and address those areas where we aren't experts, either by educating ourselves or bringing in and listening to experts, we only cut ourselves off at the knees.

Having intellectual humility means you're willing to consider everything everybody has to say and then make an honest assessment, without ego. Without intellectual humility, discernment is limited by the boundaries of your personal knowledge.

Intellectual humility is also a prerequisite for accurate self-assessment. I've always known I don't know everything, and the older I get, the more I realize how much I don't know. I'm exposed to more, and have the humility to recognize the limits of my knowledge. I also have the confidence to ask questions and to seek out expert help or advice. When your ego is wrapped up in needing to be right all the time or in maintaining the public illusion or self-deception that you already have everything all figured out, you can't risk opening yourself up to learning. Intellectual humility is the key to lifelong learning and growth.

HUMILITY + GRIT = SUCCESS

Intellectual humility and grit are the power combo of personality traits. Humility shows you your weaknesses; grit gets you working to strengthen them.

GET ON YOUR "TRYCYCLE"

Having intellectual humility and grit allows you to get—and stay—on the "trycycle" of trying, learning, and then trying smarter. The more things you can expose yourself to and try your hand at, the better off you're going to be. There's tremendous power in just starting. This is as true for huge endeavors as it is for learning a single skill. Whatever it is you want to do, get on the trycycle and pedal like crazy.

Want to be a social media star? Get on the trycycle. Try posting, learn which posts people react most strongly to, and then apply what you've learned to your next round of posts. Try, learn, try smarter. Over and over again. Start now. The best way to learn anything is by doing. You can ride your trycycle the whole way to the top. It sounds dorky, but it'll get you where you want to go.

I was never an extraordinary student until I started taking business classes. Although I was playing Division I football and running my painting business on the side, I maintained a 3.5 GPA in the College of Business exactly *because* I was running a business. While the professor was teaching us about the four P's of marketing, I wasn't thinking, "Product, price, place, and promotion are going to be on the test." I was thinking, "How can I apply that to my painting business?" I did better in school because I had a business, and my business did better because I was in school.

If you're really a business athlete, and if you're in shape physically, mentally, and spiritually, you can leverage anything you're learning this way. If you want to be a business owner, there's no better training ground than starting a business. Get paid to learn. It will take courage, humility, and grit, and that's not insignificant, but it's all you need. It will force you to learn about marketing and sales, negotiating, banking, and insurance. You'll have to learn about human resources and hiring, managing, leading, firing, and failing.

Get paid to ride your trycycle. If you're studying to be a graphic designer, get yourself on Fiverr and practice for money. If you're a computer science major, get on GitHub and start picking up work. If you're going to school for business, start one.

THE COURAGE TO START

Phil Knight, the founder of Nike, famously said, "The cowards never started, and the weak died along the way. That leaves us." If you back-engineer that outcome, it means this: if you want to be among the ones left standing, you need to develop the courage to start, the grit to stick with it, and the intellectual humility to try, learn, and try smarter.

HAVE A SIDE HUSTLE

You don't need an MBA or seed funding to start a side

hustle. If you want to be a business athlete, you need a side hustle in college that's not just punching a clock somewhere. You need to be studying marketing in class on Wednesday, then marketing your business on Saturday. Even the most prestigious MBA programs now recognize the value of this. They want you to have first worked for a few years so you have context. What you learn in theory means something practical. Reading and talking is only going to give you a certain amount of comprehension of the material. If you're actually out practicing what you learn as you're learning it and running your business, you'll see a massive increase in your mastery of that material.

My side hustle was a painting business. I picked it because I'd worked as a painter for a summer and I liked it better than wearing the dog suit at Chuck E. Cheese. Generally, the best place to look for a side hustle is somewhere that you already have access to what you need to get started, or where you have passion or experience. It doesn't have to be working experience. If your other interests or hobbies have exposed you to something interesting, you can start there—whatever lowers the barrier to entry. There are hundreds of kids as young as sixteen or seventeen who are making thousands of dollars a month going to garage sales and reselling what they find on eBay.

There's a local kid here in Huntersville, North Carolina, who has made millions selling shoes online. Why shoes?

He was a shoe guy. He just really liked shoes. He started out on YouTube, making videos about his favorites. Then he started reselling a few. Soon he was an influencer making a million bucks a year. Will this be the business he works in forever? Probably not, but he's learned about distribution and sales taxes, shipping, and customer satisfaction. And he got paid to learn it. More importantly, he's built up grit and stamina. He'll be able to work longer than the kids he went to school with. He'll be okay with not getting a mental break over the holidays. Physically, he'll have experience showing up, starting early, and working late.

Finally, and perhaps most crucially, the experience he gained through his side hustle will give him confidence, and in business, confidence equates to courage. I had safer options when I took off for Florida back in 1992. I could've tended bar or applied for jobs. I could've sat on my duff for a while as a reward for the grueling painting season I'd just come through. I didn't have any experience with disaster recovery. Packing up my truck and driving to Florida was a risk, but because of my experience starting and running a painting business, I thought I could make a go of it. I had that confidence because I had the experience. None of the great things that have happened to me in my life happened while I was sitting on the couch. You've got to get out there and make your own luck, find your own hustle.

Side hustles don't have to be based on original ideas, and

they don't have to be your thing. Shoes, clearly, were that kid's thing, but painting wasn't inherently mine until I started doing it. You can start a moving business if you have a pickup truck. You can start a painting business if you can buy a paintbrush. Then you have to be willing to do more than anyone else, harder and for longer, and to bring more value than anyone else chasing the same customers, contracts, and goals.

Just start.

The more business experience you gain, the more your discernment has to draw on. Experience informs discernment, but it's not where it gets its power. To put the force of action behind your decisions, you must be mentally, physically, emotionally, and intellectually fit, and that's what we'll tackle next.

CHAPTER SUMMARY

In addition to strong fundamentals (which everyone needs and many have), to excel as a business athlete, you need an arsenal of superpowers. Finding those places where you're likely to shine requires self-awareness and flexibility. Once you've identified your unique abilities, you must have the grit and humility to stick with the hard work of developing them. Then you need to put them into practice—trying, learning, and trying better. This isn't easy, but you can and should get paid to do it. A side hustle is the ideal training ground for your talents and a great place to start getting your growing discernment out on the field and into the game.

CHAPTER 6

INCREASE YOUR FITNESS

PUTTING DISCERNMENT'S POWER TO WORK

I was an athlete before I was a business athlete, and I believe that bringing the principles of that early training with me contributed to my success. Athletes do specific things on a regular basis—in the wee hours of the morning or evening, with others or alone—to improve their speed, strength, flexibility, and technique. It's key to their success, but I've seen too many get into the business world and fail to continue to drill down on the fundamentals of being a business athlete. Even if you've never played a sport, you'll perform better in life if you adopt the training mindset. Business athletes need to increase and safeguard their mental, physical, emotional, and intellectual health. Discernment is impacted by all four aspects of their fitness, but the critical first thing to master is the mental approach to training.

You do this by taking a serious look at your life and focusing on those aspects that increase your ability to make good decisions. It's easy to make good decisions when you're comfortable and there's nothing at stake, but for all the other times, which will be most of them, you need to increase your fitness and train yourself to overcome adversity. Your desire to start something great has to be stronger than your desire to stay comfortable.

MENTAL FITNESS

When I say "mental fitness," I'm talking about your mind's ability to think clearly and reason well, to avoid the most common thinking traps, and to approach everything with an athlete's mindset.

My daughter is an excellent example of this. When Maelee goes into the World Championship Horse Ring, she's under a lot of pressure. She competes in the most challenging class for people her age, but there's no question about whether or not the pressure is going to get to her. It's not. She embodies "Never ever panic" and "Always do more than is expected"—two of our family values. It's not unusual to see kids at this level lose their nerve and make mistakes, but that's never going to happen with Maelee—not because she's trained harder or has less at stake, but because she's been honing her mental courage and grit all her life.

She worked volunteer jobs while taking a full load of AP classes in high school and played national-caliber soccer since she was younger than that. Yes, she's physically fit, but so are all the other girls in the horse ring. Maelee has developed an inner strength that is manifested externally. She never complains, she won't make excuses, and she doesn't quit. She's all about relentlessly making progress in every aspect of her life. She's in the habit of limit-pushing, so when the pressure's on in the ring or the classroom, she's still in familiar territory. And she knows how to navigate it. It doesn't frighten her. This is the kind of mental fitness that business athletes need, the kind that comes from training yourself to go beyond your natural limits—not on those special occasions when you need the extra power, but every day, habitually.

WORDS FROM THE WISE

"The second half of a man's life is made up of nothing but the habits he has acquired during the first half."
—FYODOR DOSTOEVSKY

HOW TO MAKE DUMB DECISIONS

Think about the conditions under which you've made decisions you later regretted. When has your discernment failed? Were you tired, scared, drunk, frustrated, or just uncomfortable? What can you do to train for those conditions so that your tolerance is higher?

What discernment sinks can you simply avoid? If you get in the habit of getting enough sleep and staying (mostly) sober, you'll cut bad decisions by half. Most of my worst decisions were made drunk. I was probably under-slept for the rest. Being tired saps your motivation, and you rush to judgment instead of expending more energy to consider all the information or consequences.

Alcohol

Alcohol itself isn't a problem. The first drink is completely harmless as long as it doesn't make the second drink look like a good idea. I've often told myself I'd stop at one, but it was usually more like 1:30. Even a second drink, in and of itself, isn't that bad, unless it makes binging on food or TV or more drinks increasingly attractive until you're crushing yourself under the weight of the "fun" you're having. Don't reward yourself by treating yourself this poorly.

Alcohol also degrades the quality of your sleep, so if you're drinking tonight, you're also impacting tomorrow. Don't fall into the trap of thinking that you've worked really hard all week and deserve to kick back on the weekend. People think the weekend is two days out of seven, but it's not. It starts on Friday, sometimes before lunch, and you're still making up for it by the same time Monday. From noon Friday to noon Monday is seventy-two hours. An entire week is only 168.

The pro-level move isn't just to reward yourself by doing things like reading or spending time with your family; it's to learn how to feel good about doing the things you need to do, the things you're currently rewarding yourself for doing. What if going for a run in the morning was your reward for going for a run? I'm not suggesting you never take any downtime to recharge, but don't give back hard-earned yardage celebrating that you've gained it.

If you're not hungover Monday morning and your competitor is, you've won, and he's forfeited. You're gaining momentum while he's giving up ground. If you really want to compete directly against someone else, do it by getting in extra rounds.

Drama

When I say "drama," I'm talking about the self-inflicted injuries and chronic bad behavior in ourselves or others that we could avoid if we didn't engage with it. Beyond exhaustion and intoxication, drama is the biggest discernment-killer that you're better off avoiding. When you've fine-tuned your life and your business so that things are running smoothly, you're able to make great decisions based on a long-term vision. Drama forces your focus onto immediate, insistent issues; it makes you shortsighted. You can chart a distant course only when you're not tripping over the right now. When someone throws the drama ball at you, try to put it down and set it aside.

Obviously, I'm not talking about serious crises. Very few lives are free of at least occasional misfortune. Disease, death, and disasters are real and can, understandably, derail even the most fit business athlete. But in the same way a broken bone might take you off the field for a while, good habits and strong discipline get you back in the game. And being in good shape physically, mentally, and psychologically help you recover more quickly.

Discretionary effort—freely choosing to do more than is expected—separates the weekend warrior from the serious athlete. Optional drama pulls your focus away from what you want to be building and puts it on patching up the holes. Like too little sleep or too much to drink, drama forces you to give back hard-won yardage and forces you to start over again. It takes exponentially more energy to restart than it does to go on. Like an airplane that burns excessive fuel during the takeoff and initial climb, you're much more efficient if you maintain your cruising altitude and keep on flying.

Stop and Start

This is as simple as it is difficult: Don't do things that degrade your decision-making. Do things that increase discernment. I imagine, if you think about it, you know the activities (and lack thereof) that contribute to and detract from your ability to make good decisions, but just in case, here's a handy table for you.

Stop doing what's easy.	Start training.
Stop coasting.	Start grinding.
Stop watching.	Start reading.
Stop BLTs (bites, licks, and tastes).	Start healthy meals.
Stop complaining.	Start helping.
Stop reacting.	Start planning.
Stop stupid drama.	Start smart conversations.
Stop taking victory laps.	Start giving back.
Stop wasting time.	Start investing it.
Stop consuming.	Start creating.
Stop waiting.	Start starting.

I'm not asking you to do only those things on the right side of the chart. We all need ways to relax and blow off steam, and certainly there can be a benefit to less inhibited thinking, but when you've finished a day's work and you're looking for a way to reward yourself for what you've accomplished, picking from the right side more than the left can keep you from surrendering all the week's progress on the weekend. Learn to enjoy the progress itself. After all, you're not building a business so you can drink. You're building a business to have a business. The reward for work isn't not working.

When I talk about surrendering progress or yardage, what I really mean is giving back time. When your recreation undoes work you put time into, it surrenders the one thing you can never get back. I know people who went from $100 million in real estate equity to being $100 million in debt in 2007. Now they're back to another $100 million. Money can be won and lost and won again. Time is gone once it passes, and you can't get any more of it once it's passed. None of us know how many days we have left, and there's not much we can do about it. Sure, you can work out and eat healthy, and you should, but a bunch of skinny-ass people drop dead every day.

Time is our greatest asset and the only real currency. A dollar is a piece of paper with exactly as much value as we and the Central Bank decide it has. Right now, the US dollar is what everything is tagged against, but ten years from now, who knows? There was a time when you could buy a house on the French Riviera for a single one-ounce gold coin and another when you couldn't buy a loaf of bread in Germany for a wheelbarrow full of marks.

Killing time today leaves your future DOA.

If you avoid consumption-based activities and increase the time you invest in creation-focused ones, you'll reap returns in mental fitness that are higher-powered than most people's. But powerful minds can still fall prey to pitfalls that I call thinking traps. There are four particularly pernicious ones.

THINKING TRAPS
The "I Do It Myself" Trap

If you've ever tried to help an independent toddler get dressed in a hurry, you know how frustrating it can be. Don't be the grown-up version of that toddler. Business athletes are self-starters. We're good at getting in before everyone else and staying later, and that's great, but don't let your comfort with working alone become dogmatic. Have the humility to consult with others. You need a team of competent advisors to provide you with an adequate range of perspectives.

I struggled with this as a younger man. My rebellious nature and my pride made it very difficult for me to ask for help. I wanted to figure it all out myself and solve my problems in my own way because I thought I could do it differently, better, and faster. While that attitude, in fact, worked out in some ways, part of my maturation lay in the realization that there was no reason not to incorporate other people's perspectives.

Over time, I've learned to seek not advice, but experience. Advice—one person's opinion about what another person should do—often has dubious origins. People who have absolutely no basis for what they're saying will still advocate for "their way," a way usually driven by ego and the need to be right rather than the desire to find out what's true. And often, they're just plain wrong.

That said, there are over seven billion people on this planet and many of them have faced, in their pasts, the challenge in your immediate future. Find these people. If you do not have people in your life, in the room, and around your table who can share stories from their pasts that can provide valuable insight and inform your future, find a different room or get a bigger table.

> **Seek experience, not advice.**

Some people are nonlinear thinkers; others think analytically. Some people write, others do math. There are internally motivated people and externally motivated ones. One person can't possibly see a situation from all of these different angles; everyone has blind spots. After something from one of yours has bitten your ass a couple of times, you get much more willing to try for something closer to a 360° view of an issue. You'll reach a better decision when you put some diversity of opinion around it. Multiple perspectives should have a seat at your table; your ego should not.

It's your job to synthesize what you learn and cultivate the skill of stepping outside your personal frames of reference, biases, and experiences to look at issues from a variety of angles. Run multiple scenarios and forecast several potential outcomes. Learn to be an inclusive thinker. Listen to many, then decide alone.

Share the process; own the outcome.

The "Be Right" Trap

The desire to be liked and thought of as valuable by others isn't conceited; it's a survival mechanism. Our human programming remembers a time when becoming alienated from the tribe meant being eaten by tigers, and nobody wants that. But the need not to look stupid can translate into a paralyzing fear of being wrong. If you're overly concerned with what others are going to think, or more frightened of looking foolish than of being stagnant, it's going to impair your ability to make good decisions and will weaken your discernment.

The "Sunk Cost" Trap

This trap is the one that will get you if you try to avoid the other two traps by tacking things on at the end. If you're willing to be wrong and you get other people's input, but you don't do it until you've already put hours of research and thinking into the issue, you may well recognize you've made a mistake—you may even be able to admit it—but you're not likely to act on that knowledge.

I fell into this trap a few times early in my career. I would work really hard at something for a long time—I didn't want to look stupid in front of my team—and then I'd present my findings. Someone I'd brought into the room exactly because I knew they tended to have a different perspective would then spot something I'd missed. They'd point it out, and I'd say, "Wow, you're right." But I'd already invested so much time, energy, and even money in what I'd presented that it made it very hard to correct my course.

The "Why" Trap

I know too many people who take a "Why would I do that?" approach to tackling difficult work. What would happen if my daughter walked into the gym with that attitude? Weights are heavy. It's not going to be easy to lift them. She might think, "Why would I do that? I'm just going to put them back down," which, of course, is ridiculous. The whole point of weight training is to lift weight.

Especially early in your career, unless there is a compelling reason *not* to do something, do it. You're gaining experience and increasing your range. Like John F. Kennedy said of going to the moon, sheer difficulty can be enough of a reason to attempt something. This isn't as arbitrary as it sounds. In the same way an athlete lifts more than is comfortable, taking on projects that are beyond your ability increases your ability. Not only that, it's the only way you build courage. Practice doing hard things so that difficulty doesn't scare you. The only way you'll know you can transcend the challenges you'll face is because you already have.

Leaders have to be able to make good decisions under fire, when there's a lot to lose, and when there's no clear right answer. You train for these critical times by building a habit of putting yourself into situations that are over your head and where there's a risk that you'll fail or embarrass yourself. If you're uncomfortable with public speaking, sign up to give a talk. If meeting new people makes you nervous, go to a networking event. Maybe there's no obvious career need for you to do either of these things, but is there a reason *not* to? If the reason not to is that it scares you, that's your reason why.

Stop asking "Why?" Ask "Why not?"

You have to practice pushing your limits. Your comfort zone is bounded by your abilities, and the only way to expand it is to go beyond them. If you don't try things you're not good at, you'll never get better. Trust yourself to take chances, to be vulnerable, and to say yes. Show up. Do more than show up. Show up with purpose and passion. I don't care if it's coaching a little kids' football team or saying a few words at somebody's wedding. Build a habit of taking things on, of meeting a challenge by running right at it, of doing what scares you. Seriously. Why not?

PHYSICAL FITNESS

Saying "Why not?" to build courage is a core requirement

for training your mental fitness as a business athlete, but a well-trained thought process isn't all it takes. Discernment requires physical, emotional, and intellectual fitness as well. Like the inputs we discussed earlier, you get out what you put into a system. The quality of your thinking will never be any better than the quality of ideas you consume, and the same is true of literal consumption. Garbage in, garbage out.

If your body is unhealthy—overweight, undernourished, or out of shape—you'll tire more quickly and function less well. Because your brain is part of your body, bad physical habits also impact your thinking. Beyond flat-out toxins like alcohol and excess sugar, your brain won't perform as well as it can when you're hungry or living on junk.

It's well outside the scope of this book to set out dietary and exercise guidelines, but take a second now and evaluate your level of physical fitness. Do you get sick all the time? Does a flight of stairs wear you out? Are your feet hidden by your gut when you look down? If so, what new habits could you put in place, and which old habits do you need to get rid of?

Get enough sleep, exercise, eat well, and get a checkup every once in a while.

EMOTIONAL FITNESS

This isn't the book and I'm not the guy to teach you psychology, but it's an important part of your training, so think of what follows as Mental Health for Business Athletes 101. Obviously, if you struggle with anxiety, depression, or any other mental health issue, get the help you need from a qualified professional. But assuming a base level of health, I want to offer some pointers for increasing your emotional fitness in three key areas: your self-image, your self-worth, and your relationships.

SELF-IMAGE

Having a healthy self-image depends on maintaining congruence between what you believe and how you live. If you're doing what you believe in and living in accordance with your personal values, you'll have a healthy self-image. If you believe that living in the desert, running naked, and eating peyote is the highest (by which I mean best, not actually *high*est) form of living, but you're a Manhattanite making a killing on Wall Street in a coat and tie, your self-image won't be vital no matter how much money you make.

SELF-WORTH

You can measure your self-worth against the Abraham Lincoln quote "Whatever you are, be a good one." We all play multiple roles in life. You might be an English teacher, a football coach, a husband, and a father, or a CEO, a rower, a wife, and a mother. Self-worth comes from how you evaluate your performance in each of your roles. If our Manhattan shaman from the preceding paragraph has a poor self-image because he's not living a life that he believes in and that aligns with his values, he can still have a high degree of self-worth if he believes he's an excellent stockbroker and wears his suit well.

Choosing roles that fit who you believe you should be and then doing them well is central to the business athlete's personal emotional fitness.

RELATIONSHIPS

No amount of money or career success would mean anything to me without my family. You don't have to be a family man to be a successful business athlete, but your emotional health does depend, at least in part, on feeling connected with the people you want to have relationships with. Consider it part of your emotional fitness regimen to invest in and maintain at least a few close, personal relationships with worthwhile and inspiring people. Remember, in your friends, you see your future. It's important to get on well with what you're looking at.

INTELLECTUAL FITNESS

Read.

I almost made this section only that one word long. I really do believe that if you make a practice of reading every day, it's probably enough to maintain your intellectual health. I understand that not everyone is a reader, but I swear to you, read an hour a day every day, and you'll learn more and learn it faster. Reading is a skill, and you get better at it with practice. It expands your knowledge base, and as with money, when you gain incremental returns, the bigger the base, the greater the gains.

It would have been fun to have a one-word section, but in truth, reading isn't the only thing you can do to enhance your intellectual fitness. I've already recommended taking classes to learn basic accounting and finance, and I've advocated for enrolling in sales training as soon as you can afford to do so. If you make a commitment to lifelong learning (and you should), you can find opportunities to increase your intellectual health by learning a new skill, meeting a new person, or starting a new business. Seek to be more informed every year than you were the year before. Increase your mastery over every topic that's relevant to your business. Push yourself to understand difficult ideas.

In this and the previous chapters, we've talked about strengthening your moral core, setting goals, gaining experience, and staying healthy, which completes what you need to make good decisions in a vacuum, but that's not where we live. If you're bringing the power of a strong mind, body, heart, and intellect to the game, you've done all that you can on your own. Moving the ball from there takes a team, and that's what we'll talk about next.

CHAPTER SUMMARY

With strong values delimiting what you must have and will not tolerate, defined goals to ground your discernment, experience to inform it, and your individual talents trained to execute on it, you need to put power behind your decision-making. The business athlete puts the power of discernment to work by adopting a training mindset. You increase your mental toughness and stop doing things that contribute to bad decisions. You safeguard time as your most irreplaceable asset, and replace alcohol, drama, and other consumption-based activities with ones that create value and positive possibilities. You avoid the mental traps of refusing help, the fear of being wrong, and the "sunk cost" fallacy. You get into the habit of asking "Why not?" and you start taking smart chances. You implement good physical, emotional, and intellectual hygiene to keep your body, heart, and brain healthy, strong, and contributing to your discernment and your progress toward your goals.

CHAPTER 7

LEAD YOUR TEAM

INFLUENCING THROUGH DISCERNMENT

I got to Appalachian State in January, halfway through the school year, so at the end of my first semester, I went home for the summer. In that long-distant New Stone Age of 1989, phones were connected to walls and charged by the minute for long-distance calls. In three months of calling my girlfriend (now my wife), I ran up a ridiculous phone bill that shocked my dad, whose engineering business wasn't flourishing. I felt terrible. It was a difficult time for our family, and the state of our house reflected the same level of disrepair and deterioration, with paint peeling off the vertical wood siding. It looked like hell. I had to make up for what I had done to the phone bill, so the week before I went back to school, I painted the house.

That paint job lasted fifteen years.

Maybe it was guilt or pride, but I did it right. I scraped the whole thing down, primed the wood, and painted every inch by hand. When I got back to school, doing the same job I'd done for my dad, but for money, seemed like a logical next step. I had a roommate who'd had a more—let's say "conventional"—upbringing than I had. He had some money and a truck, and he was really sick of me borrowing his clothes. I pitched my idea to him: We'd start a side hustle painting houses, and I'd make enough to buy new clothes. We took his money, bought ladders and paint, and loaded up his truck. I convinced the lady who worked in the football office to hire us. We painted her house, did a good job, and picked up more work.

Our first summer we did maybe $8,000 in sales and met some of the property managers who handled student apartments. We got to know them over the next year and made a good enough impression that the next summer, they hired us to come in for the two weeks in May and August when the leases changed and all the students moved into or out of their apartments.

We built gigantic rolling paint pans in the school's metal shop and huge, eighteen-inch rollers that would cover wide swaths of wall. We hired additional crews and paid everyone a flat $5 an hour in cash and all the pizza they could eat. The basketball players cut in the ceilings, the wrestlers did the baseboards, and I had my first leadership role. We were charging $200 to $280 an apartment, depending on the size, but with that setup, we could crush fifteen or more of them in a day.

I recruited friends, colleagues, even the offensive coordinator of the football team—he painted for me in the summer, and I played for him in the fall—anyone who would strengthen the team, and I fired anyone who weakened it. It was my team, but it was always about "us" and what our team needed. I tried to make decisions for the good of the team, for the company, and it taught me a lot.

The second summer, we did $56,000 in sales in 1991 dollars, and $79,000 the next.

Interacting with other people, particularly from a leadership position, both requires discernment and helps to develop it. This is why, whenever opportunities come up to take a leadership role, you should always default to "yes," particularly early in your career. You'll analyze things more carefully and develop your critical skills. When you take a leadership position, whether as an employer or the captain of a football team, you establish yourself as a leader and put yourself in a position to respond to opportunities. The practice field for leadership is everywhere. If you want to be an elite business athlete, you've got to be the captain.

When my buddy called me about doing disaster recovery in Florida, it wasn't because he was trying to help me. He called me because when he got there, the company he was working for needed hundreds of additional hands. They asked him who he knew, and damned if he didn't know a guy who'd run a painting company while he was in college—a real go-getter—and they told him to call me. Demonstrating leadership and competency is what gets people to call you. You can be a great role player and that's fine, but defaulting to leadership is a hallmark of people who achieve.

> The practice field for leadership is everywhere. If you want to be an elite business athlete, you've got to be the captain.

MANIPULATION WITH GOOD INTENT

Great leaders and great manipulators are persuasive people who are able to convince others to do what they want them to. Great leaders connect with people emotionally and can change the mood of a room. Leadership is a skillset, and the only real difference between it and manipulation is the positive or negative connotation we associate with each.

Leadership, really, has no inherent value judgment. Hitler was an extraordinary leader. The well-poisoner who gossips in the parking lot can lead the joy and momentum right out of an organization. The tools of leadership, like most tools, are value-neutral.

If you run your own business, you're the boss. Your job title and your name on the checks gives you that power. It's like being a father; biology makes you that. It's an entirely different thing to be a dad. Likewise, to be a leader, you need to do more than own a business. Your leadership is apparent (or not) in how you do everything that you do. A leader is someone with

- A compelling argument for why the organization exists and why everyone in the organization needs to share a common vision.
- The ability to influence the opinions and actions of prospective customers and clients.
- Persuasive speaking and writing skills that effectively communicate their vision internally and externally.
- The ability to shape a culture of motivated individuals who are all working toward that vision.

To be a leader, you need these skills. To be a *good* leader, you need to deploy them with good intent. What guides that intent? Discernment. Good leadership is manipulation with good intent. If compelling, persuading, influencing, and motivating are all variations on the theme of manipulation, why would any ethical person want to be a leader?

Because there's no such thing as the absence of culture. When the third person walks into a room, politics emerge, and a culture starts to form. Norms get established. Biases are reinforced. If you start a business, your company *will* have a culture. It isn't optional. You can only either be intentional or negligent about it.

> **Good leadership is manipulation with good intent.**

COMPANY CULTURE

If you don't deliberately manipulate your environment, you let the lowest common denominator drag everyone down. Good leaders lead, not to get better work from blindly obedient people, but because they have the discernment to know people need a great place to work and an inspiring vision to follow. This is the positive intention at the core of all good leadership.

It's also what makes it difficult.

A good leader is principled, and people with principles are, almost by definition, not easygoing folks who everyone always likes to be around. We can be abrasive. And where that's the friction of principles, not bad manners, it's a good thing. Leadership means placing yourself in opposition to anyone who resists the positive intent you're trying to implement. You company's culture is something you have to deliberately create and curate, and it, like everything else, starts with values.

A company's culture is a closed environment, it's the ecosystem inside the organization, and alignment with its values is the price of admission. If a person isn't on board with your company's values, they don't get through the front gate. Once they're inside, it can be assumed that everyone is operating from a shared set of values. That creates a bond between people, a sense of community, and the foundations of company culture.

Building up from there, a culture is composed of shared stories—a curated organizational memory that reflects and reinforces the values everyone shares. In addition to shared stories, many cultures have a shared unique language. It's not unusual for people to have nicknames inside their organization, many of which are often tied to stories about the thing they did that led to their rechristening.

> "Culture guides behavior and provides a sense of identity, stability, and organizational boundaries. It is the organization's memory. You must work harder at it than anything else."
>
> —HERB KELLEHER, CO-FOUNDER OF SOUTHWEST AIRLINES AND AUTHOR OF *NUTS!*

SHARED STORIES

A thriving culture creates a virtuous cycle by creating a values-based, mission-driven bond between people. When you celebrate and reward behavior that is consistent with your company's values and mission, you create stories. Those stories unite people and change the way they see themselves and the organization. This, in turn, improves the company's brand, which raises its performance and motivates people to act in ways that are consistent with its values and mission. Before the internet and workplace-focused sites like Glassdoor, a company's brand was whatever its marketing department said it was, and culture was the (often ugly) secret life lived behind its closed doors. Nobody knew what it was like to work for any given company except the people who worked there. Now, culture and brand have practically merged. Today, brand is culture on display.

People associate who you are with what you do. Companies like Southwest and Zappos are successful, in part, because of the reputation their culture has. Sales at many big-box stores, in contrast, have suffered as a result of what people have learned about the way these companies treat their employees.

I have a friend who says the only reason she dropped her Sam's Club membership and picked up one at Costco was her perception that Costco pays its people well and offers benefits. I doubt Toms would sell as many shoes if they weren't matching each pair sold with one given away. Google initially differentiated its search engine from others with their "Don't be evil" motto. Companies publicize their values and culture, and consumers who share those values support them with their business. Having a good culture is good business, which isn't the reason to have a great culture, but it's the reason it's getting done.

> **Brand is culture on display.**

PEOPLE

A strong culture is based on values and designed to serve your mission, but ultimately, it's built by and composed of people. I credit AdvantaClean's strong culture with the unusually low rate of call center turnover we maintained. The relationships forged between our call center staff and our franchise owners were part of our cultural "secret sauce," and the improved rates of retention benefited both sides of the equation.

We paid people well, and I'm sure that's part of the picture, but we also made it very clear that every employee was part of the company family. If we held a picnic, we made sure that the call center employees could be outside with everyone else, even if they needed to have their laptops and cell phones with them to keep answering incoming calls. When prospective franchisees came for discovery days, they met, shook hands with, and sat down to lunch with everyone in the organization, including the call center staff. We didn't just tell them they mattered. We showed them. It's the decent thing to do, and I would have done it even if it didn't save us money in having to constantly find, vet, hire, and train new people. It felt like the right thing to do, and when I ultimately sold the business, I made sure that everyone, down to the last employee, received something meaningful.

We had a Franchisee of the Year recently who, because of a family crisis, wasn't going to be able to attend the award ceremony. His partner was going to accept it for him, but someone inside the organization decided that there was a better way to express our values. He or she—I don't know who it was—went to great lengths to get a camera and crew to the guy's house with a remote linkup so that he could accept the reward in real time in front of his peers in the convention hall. The next year, he and his wife came up and danced together at the convention. I don't remember what else happened that night—what I spoke about or what we ate. It was such an emotional thing, and I'd had nothing to do with any of it. Other people in the organization had created it all, but it's a story you could tell with authenticity and sell a franchise on. It beautifully captures who we are as an organization. It tells people that if they join us, these are the kinds of things that will be celebrated.

TRUST

To lead people, you need a track record of good decisions to inspire their trust and confidence. Personal relationships and loyalty to you as an individual will only get you so far, and usually only when your company is small enough for you to have one-on-one relationships with every member of your team. If you have great discernment and a reputation for making decisions that are thoughtful, consistent, and fair, people are more likely to give you the benefit of the doubt and believe that you're leading them in the right direction with the right intent. When people believe they're getting great rewards on their investments of time and energy in a company, they repay it in care, loyalty, and performance. They'll do their best for the company when they know the company cares what's best for them.

Inside such a culture, trust is high, and in high-trust environments, decisions can be made much more quickly. Great company cultures allow for high-quality, high-velocity decision-making. In such environments, decisions can be examined, tested, and probed from a diversity of perspectives by multiple people at a pace that arrives at the best possible decision in the shortest amount of time.

Trust needs to extend to all of your business dealings. Deals that would normally take two years can be concluded in a month when both parties are confident that everything will be delivered exactly as promised. Due diligence and legal documents can provide some certainty in the face of distrust or unfamiliarity, but when people know and trust you, deals go forward at the speed of trust, not the speed of covering your butt. Good, well-considered agreements up front head off bad disagreements down the road, so it's important to do all your negotiating up front.

> **Good agreements at the start head off bad disagreements down the road.**

You have to not only create but also safeguard your company's culture. Once it's lost, it's nearly impossible to get back. This means responding to value breaches, if and when they happen, before they establish new norms. Once anything that runs counter to the company's values is overlooked or becomes part of a new normal, people lose their trust, and nothing erodes a culture more quickly than distrust. I've asked countless people what made a culture they'd been a part of go bad, and the answer is always some variation on "What management said was going to happen didn't."

LEADERSHIP

Certainly, creating and protecting a thriving company culture is a critical part of any leader's job. You're not leading if no one follows. To lead, you must be able to influence not just the culture, but the individuals who comprise it. Leadership is the discerning exercise of influence.

I had this lesson reframed for me by social media megastar Devan Kline, whose advice I sought out. I've found that my concern for other people's opinion of me makes social media a struggle. I want people to like what I post, but the internet isn't known for its supportive comments and patience. Devan pointed out that influence means the ability to cause change. And people don't like change. They can get pretty angry, in fact, with anyone who tries to change their minds. But if you're not trying to effect change, you're not trying to influence or lead, and you might as well make an online conga line and give each other virtual back rubs. Leadership *is* influence.

Your influence, or lack thereof, is visible in everything your company is or does. It's what creates and protects the culture (which is now nearly synonymous with brand), but the discernment of that influence is most visible in the strength of a leader's teams.

BUILDING STRONG TEAMS

Human beings are tribal animals with a strong desire to be around the people we know, like, and trust. They can be brought together under a well-intended leader to make progress toward a worthy ideal. Inside a culture that fosters such positive feelings, people feel happy and accountable to one another. They form teams and strive mightily to do great things for their teammates. It's the vibe that builds the tribe.

Great leaders assemble powerful teams by attending to all the necessary pieces. Great leaders create a culture bonded by shared values with clearly defined, inspiring goals. They exercise the discernment necessary to execute on those goals from a place of strong fundamentals and highly developed talents. A great leader powers those skills and abilities with high levels of mental, physical, emotional, and intellectual vitality. In that environment, great leaders build teams that are internally motivated by their commitment to one another and to the group, and they protect those teams by establishing a meritocracy and a cadence.

It's the vibe that builds the tribe.

Establish a Meritocracy

Putting the right people in the right roles has to be based on people's talents and skills with everyone serving in their highest-value position, not on seniority or nepotism. There's only one ball on the field, and not everybody gets to throw it. Even if your dad tells me you went to quarterback camp over the summer, if you're not the best fit for what we want to do and for what the team needs, then "tight end" better start sounding pretty good to you.

For a company to be truly merit-based, its leader needs to make clear from the beginning that people can be moved to different positions, and that the duties associated with a position can be shifted based on assessments of their performance. Regular and universal performance assessments, in contrast to entitlements like seniority, need to be baked into the culture from the outset. Everybody has to be assessed, and you have to be consistent and objective in that evaluation and focused on creating the best possible team. To do that gracefully, in a culture-promoting, trust-building, and principled way, you need to be very clear about how such decisions are made and explained.

Success in one role should be a prerequisite for mobility in an organization. I want people who will push through, succeed, and ask for the next job, not people who want to change positions, peeking around the corner for something easier. Not all jobs are created equal in terms of the effort or difficulty required. In the same way that athletes who overcome obstacles raise the bar, good leaders reward and challenge people with new opportunities to learn, earn, grow, and prove themselves. Now that's progress, baby!

Establish a Cadence

You need the right people in the right positions, and you need them working at the right pace. Even huskies don't run the Iditarod with their tongues hanging out the whole time. They occasionally stop to sleep and eat frozen fish. You need to create times when your entire team is sprinting together, and times for them to catch their breath. The fish are optional.

Even the toughest training includes recovery days. Establishing a cadence should be a part of your strategic planning process. If you need to launch a new project, it's fine to plan for a seven-week sales push, but you want to follow that up with a week of lighter work and lower expectations followed by a shorter, three-week push. Cadence matters for everyone, which is part of why everyone in the company participates in events like our Spring Fling picnic. It's particularly critical for sales teams. You can only go full speed part time. If you don't give people breaks, they'll never reach capacity. Like athletes, have your people sprint in intervals and build in recovery time.

CHAPTER SUMMARY

Increasing your discernment by defining your values, planning your direction, building your fundamental skills, developing your unique abilities, and strengthening your mental, physical, emotional, and intellectual fitness is great, but nowhere is it more powerful and more powerfully advanced that by taking on leadership roles. A leader with discernment will manipulate people with positive intent to create a thriving and productive culture of trust protected by meritocratic practices and maintained by a deliberately paced cadence.

CHAPTER 8

MAINTAIN YOUR GAINS

ESTABLISHING DISCERNMENT-
ADVANCING PRACTICES

If I gave you $500 and told you to turn it into $1,000 by tomorrow, you'd have to work pretty hard or take some very big risks. If you wanted to lose ten pounds by the weekend, it would be about all you did between now and then. Incremental steps taken every day are the only path to some destinations. Compound interest creates wealth, and true wealth is hard to come by any other way.

Likewise, we need to give thought to how we invest our time. An hour is made up of the same sixty minutes for everyone. You can exchange that hour for anything from an extra hour of *Family Feud* to a life-changing conversation. How you spend your time determines its value. An hour spent on a great book simply has more value than one spent watching TV. And just like smart investments of money, smart investments of time compound with interest.

Unlike a savings account, however, when you put time and effort into building a good habit, it doesn't simply continue to increase in value. The friction of the daily grind wears you down. And as much as nature abhors a vacuum, entropy abhors a habit. Of course, you have the right to be mediocre, but "average" is one data point above "you suck." If you want to avoid suckage, you have to default to action, take opportunities, and avoid excuses. You have to resist the daily friction and the pull of entropy. A consistent pressure toward good habits over time is how you'll collect the wins, while bad habits compound your losses just as quickly. What's more, bad habits can kill you.

Of course, you can't get healthy in two days. But exercise an hour a day for a month and you'll start to notice the difference. The same goes for becoming wealthy and wise. Start spending your time learning, and that investment will pay off.

You get twenty-four hours in a day. One way or another, you're going to spend all of them. Like an inn whose vacant rooms can never be recovered because the innkeeper's inventory expires every midnight, when you go to bed tonight, today's hours will be gone. What value will you have exchanged those hours for? How much interest will you have earned on that time? I'm going to give you some investment advice, and I'm not going to put a bunch of qualifiers on it like the financial guys do: Invest in experiences, education, and relationships. In the previous chapters, I've taught you how to how to make all those investments, and in this final chapter, I'll teach you how to practice what you've learned to maintain your gains.

COLLECT EXPERIENCES

The next time you're having a conversation with someone, ask them how they ended up in their career, how they met their spouse, or why they live where they do. I don't know them and I don't know you, but I'd bet cash money that their answers will hinge on something coincidental. If you hadn't been in the same church group, maybe you never would have met your wife. You might be married, but not to her. You might have kids, but not the ones you love so much now.

What are the odds you'll go to a college in a state you've never visited? How many adult professional football players do you guess weren't exposed to football as kids? Never in the history of the world has a kid started speaking English who grew up hearing only Mandarin. Our experiences—good and bad—don't just shape us, but they also form the boundaries of what's possible. Having more experiences means having more possibilities. So have a ton of them, but choose them for yourself.

I've noticed that many kids today suffer from too many good options. They have programmed sports, programmed classes—programmed lives! There is a benefit to figuring out big uncertainties yourself and being comfortable feeling untethered. It's almost an advantage of being disadvantaged. Kids whose parents have provided them with three great options for after-school activities, three great options for college, and three great options for vacation destinations have never had any white space in their lives. They may collect a raft of great experiences, but they won't have had the experience of taking a chance on something they came up with themselves or of having an adventure of their own choosing. They might know what safety feels like, but not how it feels to walk a tightrope with no net. If progress is a prerequisite for fulfillment and happiness, too many good backup options can create an impediment to doing something great all by yourself, of your own creation and your own choice.

This ties back to the idea we talked about in Chapter 6. Especially when you're young, anytime the chance to expand your range of experience shows up, your question has to be "Why not?" Do I want to join the team? Why not? Do I want to be captain? Same question. Don't wonder if you're qualified; don't ask why you should spend the extra time and energy doing more work. Don't ask why. Ask why not. Sometimes, there's a good answer, but "Why not?" is the right question for building discernment.

- Do I want to stay out all night drinking? Why not? Because the morning may bring opportunities I don't want to miss, and most of my worst choices have been made drunk. Those are good reasons not to.
- Do I want to wake up early and read for an hour before my workout? Why not? I'm tired and bed is comfortable. That's not a good reason. Get off your butt.
- Should I go to that conference? Why not? It's where everybody in my industry will be, but I don't know exactly what I'm going to get out of it. That's a dumb reason. You know if you don't go, you'll get nothing. Get in the car or on the plane, and show up.

You may have heard that learning what to say no to is a key skill of discernment, and it's true, especially as you get older. Because of the compounding interest on the hours already invested, by the time you're my age, every sixty seconds is worth exponentially more. One of my hours comes with the weight of everything I've learned and experienced up to now, so I'm more judicious about how I spend it. Life is like toilet paper; the closer you get to the end, the faster it goes.

PRACTICE LEADING

You can argue for days about whether talents are created by nature or nurture, but ultimately, I'm not sure it matters. The bottom line is you have to work your butt off to develop leadership. Most of the leaders I know are unhappy when they're between gigs with no team to lead. Maybe we all have an oversized need to be liked and admired, but I think it's more likely that people just like doing what they do well. Either way, nobody's born with discernment—babies are ridiculous decision-makers—and you don't get it in a single, mighty leap.

Discernment and leadership are acquired slowly through small daily steps. It requires deliberate practice. So, especially in your twenties and thirties, take every possible opportunity to lead: a club, a fund drive, or a sports team. Just get your hours in.

> Discernment is a cumulative asset.

CREATE POWER HABITS

If compound interest is the eighth wonder of the world, habits are the compound interest of life. The particular genius of compound interest is that it requires only a small initial investment. If you spend only half an hour five days a week working out, you'll be in fantastic shape. Besides, you already spend more time than that each day just figuring out where you left your phone. A habit of regular exercise and good nutrition returns a longer life. A habit of hard work and frugal spending returns wealth. But perhaps the three best investments you can make to compound the quality of your life and improve your discernment are those in the books you read, the conversations you have, and the people you meet.

THE BOOKS YOU READ

I've talked about the massive benefits I've accrued from reading, and the best way to really capitalize on its power is to create a daily reading habit. If you read for an hour every weekday, at the end of the year, you will have read for 260 hours. Do that every year for ten years, and you'll be exponentially smarter and more knowledgeable. Each good book you read adds to the value of every other book you've read. You begin to see the similarities and differences between thinkers on a given topic, and that exposure and the process of comparison can't help but increase your discernment.

THE CONVERSATIONS YOU HAVE

Invest in the quality of your conversations, particularly with the people who matter the most to you because—say it with me now—*show me your friends, and I'll show you your future*. Build a habit around having regular, thoughtful, and substantive talks with your family members and business partners. If you're the average of the five people you spend the most time with, you must choose these people wisely.

You can raise your collective average by pushing the conversations you have beyond the ordinary, day-to-day things. Discuss what you're reading. Ask about the experiences others have had. High-quality conversations are the way relationships evolve, and if you're making the right level of investment, relationships deepen over time. You don't reap the greatest value of good coaching in the first season; it builds incrementally from season to season. Over time, a coach is more able to tailor coaching to the individual athlete, and the athlete places higher levels of trust in what he hears. It's only within an established relationship that real transfer of meaning and sharing of worldview can occur.

THE PEOPLE YOU MEET

Go out of your way to meet inspiring and interesting people. You're not going to find them walking by your window. If you want to catch tuna, you don't take your bait and rod to the pond. There are no tuna there. Create a habit of leaving shore and putting yourself out where the tuna are.

Unlike fish, you need to catch hundreds of people to find one you want to take home. You may have to meet a thousand people to find the hundred who will matter most to you.

If you're just starting out, you might not get to meet many of the bigger fish or have much to offer in return if you do. That's fine. I certainly didn't know any business titans when I was painting houses. Find people your own age who are as hungry as you are. Look for people who are just ahead of where you want to be and get to know them. In ten years, it'll feel like you started together. Help the next guy up.

After he put himself through college running the painting business I'd started, my brother Mike wound up as the CFO of the Carolina Panthers. He was on the team that led the sale of the Panthers from the Richardson family to a new group of owners about the time I sold AdvantaClean. After a nine-month transition, he came back to create Dudan Partners with me. Thirty years after we started in college, we're working together again, building our next new adventure.

Successful people are interested in people. I used to have the experience of admiring people from a distance, but once I was moving in the same circles, I found they were as interested in me as I was in them. Curiosity about others is a hallmark of the kind of mind that goes on to accomplish great things. Just make sure that you have the knowledge base, the experiences, and the stories to make someone's investment in you worth their time. Meeting people is only a growth amplifier if it returns value to both people, and people who've put in their time to develop their discernment recognize it in others. Work on yourself to bring value to others.

I can close a multimillion-dollar deal in a few hours, but it took me twenty-five years to cultivate that skill. When I'm on the phone with someone high enough up the food chain to do those kinds of deals, we recognize each other. We may be from different industries—in fact, as I move into advising businesses on the practice of franchising, we always are—but we're each an expert in our own domain. We have the discernment to recognize discernment and the experience to recognize experience. When I connect with someone on that level, I know everything I need to about them, and they know the same about me.

Work on yourself to bring value to others.

Whenever I meet someone new, subconsciously or even consciously, I evaluate their breadth of knowledge, their depth of experience, and their intellectual humility—in short, I take a measure of their discernment. That doesn't mean I expect, or would even enjoy, people who know everything I do. I'm an expert in my field, so I recognize expertise, even in areas where I have very little knowledge.

When that happens, I ask a ton of questions.

People generally like sharing their expertise and respond well to intelligent questions; I know I do. Additionally, asking interesting, thoughtful questions is a great way to demonstrate discernment. This is not the same as asking someone to simply give you all their knowledge when you have nothing with which to reciprocate. Don't do that. Instead, read and learn more to bring to the table. Where there's a discernment disconnect, where people perceive a lack of experience, knowledge base, access, rigor, or background to enlighten them and help inform their own decisions, they invest less in the relationship.

This discernment is almost the inverse of a first impression. We're all subject to being biased by our first impression, but it's a poor guide and one you should work against, rather than be led by. Put in the time to get an accurate assessment. Assume the best, then test for it.

THE CALENDAR HABIT

If you accept that it's the books you read, the conversations you have, and the people you meet that make the best investments of your time, you'll find you need to manage your time using a calendar more than a task list. If there's task-oriented work to do, fine. Put it on a list, and get it done in the time you don't have calendared for meeting with people. We all have taxes to file, paperwork to do, and email to answer, but the higher percentage of people-oriented things you have on your calendar, the more opportunities you'll have for the conversations and people who will increase your discernment. And anytime you can speak one-to-many or have a conversation with an entire room, you get a bonus return on your investment of time.

When I was first getting started in business, I managed to a task list, but when I switched over to ordering my life and work by a calendar, I became infinitely more successful almost immediately. It allowed me to hire an assistant to take over many of the tasks on my list, which freed me up even more to focus on the people parts of my business.

Be quick but not in a hurry.

When you're task-oriented, it's easy to start feeling rushed and panicked that you're not doing enough. When you manage to a calendar, if you trust the process, you can execute with confidence, in a workman-like fashion, being quick about it but not rushing. It's when you're in a hurry that mistakes get made. Being rushed is like being in a sack. You can flail around all you want, but you're not going to get anywhere fast. Get out of your hurry, and you'll go faster.

Don't expect the payoffs to be immediate or linear. Your application of discernment-building habits, coupled with your tireless pursuit of excellence, will reward you over time. In tough times, you may feel like you're running up a muddy, slippery hill, making little progress and even backsliding. But remain steadfast. Breakthroughs are often preceded by breakdowns, and we often gain yardage in big chunks, only after consistent pressure has been applied to the right things over time. Likewise, compound interest doesn't accrue overnight. It takes time, and you have to be patient. When you're working on the right things, you don't have to rush. Cumulative gains are happening—and can only happen—over time.

THE SELF-REFLECTION HABIT

One powerful way to compound your planning, doing, learning, and experiencing is to have a habit of regular self-scrutiny. I've talked before about the importance of being self-aware, but it isn't a static trait. You need to build self-reflection into your life. Establish a cadence of regular self-reflection and honest feedback from others for both your business and personal development. The unexamined life, as Socrates observed thousands of years ago, is not worth living.

The habit of self-assessment and self-correction is a hallmark of greatness. The most successful businesspeople I see are the ones who try out new tools and techniques. Often, these innovative tools were taught to their team or implemented by their staff. As leaders, they took it upon themselves to learn the same new techniques. It takes great discernment to recognize when a better way of doing things comes along, and even greater courage and humility to admit that your way isn't always the best.

A great athlete who feels like he's in a slump or starts missing free throws needs discernment and self-reflection to get back on track. In the same way, a leader needs to be able to self-correct in response to their own reflection, feedback, or new information.

If there's a problem in their organization, a great business athlete will always start with self-assessment. They'll ask themselves questions like these: "Where am I part of this problem?" "Did I facilitate adequate communication around that issue?" "Did I allocate enough resources?" "Was I clear about what was expected?" Always and above all else, take responsibility. Know that you are fully responsible for the outcomes in your world. Do not cloud your introspection with excuses, blame, or other nonproductive evasions.

Develop the habit of intellectual humility, the ability to see yourself objectively, and the willingness, without ego, to make course corrections. Only with these attributes in place can the "stop doing" process kick in and allow you to change direction in the face of imminent danger. This has a compound impact: on your credibility and that of those around you, and on the valuable time invested by you and those you lead. Today, such course corrections are called "pivots." Not too long ago, they were just screw-ups.

It's your life to build, so go ahead and own it.

THE 10 PERCENT HABIT

Often, the difference between success and mediocrity is only that last fraction of the distance to the finish line, the final 10 percent that takes 50 percent of your effort. Students can do some of their homework, pay attention most of the time, and throw down a C+ or a B- without much effort, assuming they are reasonably intelligent. Getting that high A—say 95 or above—takes more than twice as much effort. But that's where the real money is; it's in the slim margin between "great" and "exceptional." And it takes more effort than many are willing to give. In other words, it takes as much energy to go from okay to great as it does to get from nothing to okay. But it's worth it. When you put in twice the effort to close that final distance, you become the best of the best. The last 10 percent is where your interest starts to compound and cumulative benefits accrue.

Life is not a la carte. You can't pick and choose, or order only dessert. Once you realize everything that's required to win, if you want that victory, you must do everything it takes. Putting in that extra effort elevates you above the common swirl to an entirely different playing field. You have to fight with yourself every day to double down on your effort and earn that last 10 percent.

THE NINETY-DAY PLAN

I've watched a lot of new franchisees over the years, people who buy a franchise hoping to level up their wealth and their results, who then try to operate the business exactly the way they were operating previously. The further along people get in their business careers, the worse this tendency gets. People will fold themselves nearly in half trying to fit everything into the systems they're used to and the processes they're comfortable with, rather than grow into something new.

To address this in AdvantaClean franchises, I created a ninety-day plan. I wrote it up on a whiteboard in about an hour, my team copied it down and put it into a binder, and it made a difference.

Here's the big secret: When you start something new, how you operate after ninety days will become your default way of operating in the future. After ninety days of a new diet, a new job, a new fitness regimen, or a new relationship, patterns are established and everything going forward is just change management. If you put in the additional focus and extra work up front, you'll be grounded in the fundamentals and in as close to an ideal position as is possible.

I could make some educated guesses about why this three-month period is so powerful, but ultimately, it doesn't really matter. All that matters is that it is, and you can channel that power to your advantage or let it pass you by. Putting it to work for you is simple, if not easy:

- Step 1: Invest time in researching, investigating, and asking the right questions to know what excellence looks like.
- Step 2: Do that.

For example, let's imagine you've just gotten your realty license and you're getting ready to go into business. Before your first day, find the best Realtors and study what they do. Figure out how they start their day, how they handle leads, how they close sales, how they manage their calendar, and how they get their listings. Ask yourself: *If I were already the best Realtor in the world, what would my habits be?* And then start doing those things. Do not compromise on any of them. Allow yourself no deviance from the ideal in your first ninety days.

ADVANTACLEAN'S NINETY-DAY PLAN

My ninety-day plan for AdvantaClean franchisees took them from 7:30 in the morning to 5:00 at night with specific tasks slotted into particular weeks, and others assigned to designated days.

Every Friday, for example, was Follow-Up Friday. First, I had them identify different sectors within their territory that they needed to build relationships with: insurance, industrial hygiene, real estate and property management, and various trades like plumbing and HVAC. Each of these communities where they needed to be known, liked, and trusted were assigned a single week. From Monday through Thursday, the people in the plan had to make sales calls. Follow-Up Friday gave them a day proximate enough to the first meeting to continue a conversation. They could meet people for breakfast, lunch, dinner, or drinks in less formal contexts on the Friday after their first weekday contact. It was such a great get-up-and-running plan that nobody ever completed it. They got too busy running.

YOUR NINETY-DAY PLAN(S)

Right now, make your own ninety-day plan:

- Step 1: Ask yourself what excellence looks like.
- Step 2: Find a successful model or two, and learn how they do what they do. Then do it.

This whole book has been about giving you an inside view of how I do things, and I'll summarize them all for you here in two ninety-day plans.

Plan 1

Watch for discernment in action. It can be hard to tell which of the many decisions you'll make in your lifetime will be as pivotal as my casually made decision to go down to Florida. Remember that your friends determine your future. Choose the people you keep closest for their positive impact and superior discernment. Watch and learn. Practice using a better, more deliberate process than the usual one. Remember that there are no absolutes, just probabilities, but the number and quality of your actions will affect your outcomes.

Define your core values and get very clear about them. With a strong moral core, many possible options will be excluded on the grounds that they don't provide what you must have or do involve something you will not tolerate. Make your values visible—on the wall and in every one of your actions. Make sure that they're virtuous and that they drive behaviors that build equity in your relationships, reputation, and health. You can, and probably should, define different core values for your life and your business, but make sure you have integrity across them all.

You can't decide where you come from, but if you don't decide where to go, you'll never get there. Set values-screened and vision-guided goals, and have a strategy that's at least one step up from Nickelback. Order your priorities. Put your money and your time into them, and plan your path in a series of ninety-day missions. Don't expect that path to run a straight line, but commit to it anyway. Make this your first one.

Exercise discernment in the skills you develop and drill on. Cover the basics and add others as you discover you need them. Or just add them for fun. Learn sales by investing in training, learn basic accounting and finance by enrolling in classes, and read up on HR and marketing.

Develop the self-awareness to identify your strengths, and train them to be stronger while maintaining flexibility in your thinking. Develop grit. Your ninety-day plans will test it. Do not fail. And when you don't, be humble anyway. You're a long way from done. All great business athletes ride the trycycle every day of their lives. Find yourself a side hustle and try, learn, and try smarter.

Put your increasing discernment to work auditing your mental, emotional, physical, and intellectual health. Stop doing the things that erode both health and discernment, and start spending your time like the limited, irretrievably shortening, and ultimate currency it is. Stay out of the most common mental traps, get enough sleep, eat right, and exercise. Make sure you're living in accordance with your values and up to your standards. Take excellent care of the most important relationships in your life. Read.

Take every leadership opportunity that presents itself. Create others. Stepping into leadership roles puts you in opportunity's path. From there, learn to manipulate with good intent. Create, maintain, and defend a culture in which people share stories, feel valued for who they are, and have a high level of trust in you and in each other. Never stop earning that trust. Build it into your teams by making them meritocracies and establishing their cadence to include times of rigor and of respite.

Once you've done these things, keep doing them. Carry your discernment-enhancing practices forward into your next ninety days. Build habits that compound your investments of time, and go out of your way to have new experiences. Lead. Invest heavily in conversation, people, and books. Use a calendar to make sure you manage to message and create a practice of regular self-reflection, assessment, and growth. Having realized everything it takes to be successful, do all of it. Spend the second 50 percent of your effort to cross the 10 percent gap. Try new things, and when you do, assume that how you operate after ninety days is how you'll operate going forward, so strive for early excellence. Try new things, start a new business, and do it with a rigorous first ninety-day plan locked into place.

Plan 2

For your first ninety days in a new business, you want to be creating great habits and muscle memory. You want to be executing and learning, and connecting with the people who are going to be critical to your success.

Whatever industry your side hustle is, identify the relevant communities. Who do you need to build relationships with? What are your target markets? Once you've identified the most important ones, ask yourself what you have to offer these people. Why would they want to engage with you? What's your unique selling proposition for each group?

On the first Monday of your ninety days, you start locating people in the first of the communities you identified. Start on Google and LinkedIn. Make appointments to talk in person or by phone during the upcoming week. Set yourself a target of four connections a day. Bring the best of what you have to offer to every meeting or call, and on Friday follow up. Over the weekend, think back over the past week, evaluate your performance, and plan ways to do even better in the next week.

In your second week, follow the same schedule with the next community on your list, making whatever refinements to your technique you've discovered you need. Follow this regimen for three weeks, and in the fourth week, change up your cadence and take something like a recovery week. Don't stop putting in the hours, but take a break from making sales calls.

At the end of ninety days, you will have locked in great work habits, made connections in every relevant community, and improved your interactions. You'll have everything you need to keep improving your discernment and reaping the rewards of increasingly improved decision-making on your next ninety-day mission.

CONCLUSION

Discernment is a principled, effective, experience-informed process for powerful decision-making. It's what lifts leaders above mediocrity and puts business athletes on a path to a great life through better decisions. It is the application of your accumulated wisdom to your current situation to improve the probability of a desired outcome.

I said marrying Traci was the best decision of my life, but maybe the most life-altering was the one I made when I slunk back home after a failed year at the University of Northern Iowa. At that point, my life could have gone several ways, and only one of them was good. The good one was, as is so often the case, the most difficult, but I've never had a moment of regret for a drop of the blood spilled or sleep lost by taking it. I'm a business athlete because in that moment, what I had learned as an athlete put me on the path to business school and business success.

I wrote this business athlete's regimen in part because discernment is the difference that made the difference in my life. A few good decisions can be all that it takes to turn your life around. I didn't have much in the way of discernment when I came back from Iowa, but if you've ever had a great coach, or if you are willing to let me coach you, it's all you'll need to get started.

Good luck. Get to work.

BOOK RECOMMENDATIONS

As I mentioned in the text, reading has been an important part of my personal and professional development. Now that you have finished my book, here are a few others that have made an impression upon me, and to whose pages I have returned time and again to inform my most important decisions.

ON PERSONAL DEVELOPMENT
- *The On-Purpose Person* by Kevin W. McCarthy
- *The 5 Love Languages* by Gary Chapman
- *Magic Words* by Tim David
- *The Present* by Spencer Johnson

- *Stress Is a Choice* by David Zerfoss
- *How We Decide* by Jonah Lehrer
- *The Talent Code* by Daniel Coyle
- *Mindset* by Carol S. Dweck

ON MOTIVATION

- *The 10X Rule* by Grant Cardone
- *Bounce* by Keith McFarland
- *Drive* by Daniel H. Pink
- *Principles* by Ray Dalio
- *Wins, Losses, and Lessons* by Lou Holtz
- *Grit* by Angela Duckworth
- *Man's Search for Meaning* by Viktor E. Frankl
- *Stop Starting Over* by Devan Kline
- *Start with Why* by Simon Sinek
- *The Subtle Art of Not Giving a F*ck* by Mark Manson

ON STRATEGY

- *Good to Great* by Jim Collins
- *Mastering the Rockefeller Habits* by Verne Harnish
- *Traction* by Gino Wickman
- *Predictably Irrational* by Dan Ariely

ON LEADERSHIP

- *The Speed of Trust* by Stephen M.R. Covey

- *Winning with People* by John C. Maxwell
- *Reach* by John Rotche
- *The Servant* by James C. Hunter
- *Revolutionize Teamwork* by Eric Coryell
- *Tribal Leadership* by Dave Logan, John King, and Halee Fischer-Wright
- *Hey, Coach!* by Jeff Dudan

ON ORGANIZATIONAL ASCENSION

- *The Checklist Manifesto* by Atul Gawande
- *Double Double* by Cameron Herold
- *Grow Smart, Risk Less* by Shelly Sun
- *The Pumpkin Plan* by Mike Michalowicz
- *The Franchise MBA* by Nick Neonakis
- *Blue Ocean Strategy* by W. Chan Kim and Renee Mauborgne
- *The Compound Effect* by Darren Hardy
- *Rework* by Jason Fried and David Heinemeier Hansson
- *The Highest Calling* by Lawrence Janesky
- *How Google Works* by Eric Schmidt and Jonathan Rosenberg

BY FAVORITE AUTHORS

Read anything by these authors.

Malcolm Gladwell

- **The Tipping Point**
- **Outliers**
- **Blink**
- **David and Goliath**

Chip and Dan Heath

- **Switch**
- **Decisive**
- **Made to Stick**

Patrick Lencioni

- **Death by Meeting**
- **The Advantage**
- **Getting Naked**
- **The Four Obsessions of an Extraordinary Executive**
- **The Five Temptations of a CEO**
- **The Five Dysfunctions of a Team**

FAVORITE RECORDINGS FROM YOUTUBE

- *The Strangest Secret* by Earl Nightingale—31 Minutes
- *Principles for Success* by Ray Dalio—28 Minutes

ACKNOWLEDGMENTS

Experiences shape our thinking, inform our perspective, and enrich our lives. People are the pathway thereto. To all the people along my path, I am forever in your debt.

To my family for creating the universe that matters more to me than anything: Traci, Zack, Jack, Maelee, LeeAnn, Bob, Mike, Kristina, Casey, Jacob, and Alena; Russ, Suzy, Max, and Maddie; Billy, Evelyn, Jennifer, Hannah, Olivia, Lillian, and Amelia; Leo, Mae, Vic, and of course Grandma "Red" Louise.

To my coaches for showing me how to lead and inspire: Head Coaches Tom Mueller, Ron Creiger, Tom Cerasani, John Eliasik, and Coach Jerry Moore and the amazing coaching staffs at Appalachian State University, William Rainey Harper Junior College, and Schaumburg High School.

To the business athletes and mentors—too many to mention but represented here by David Zerfoss, Dan Luby, David McKinnon, John Rotche, Charlie Chase, Rory O'Dwyer, Shannon Wilburn, Devan Kline, Nick Neonakis, Shelly Sun, Catherine Monson, Lane Fisher, Brad Fishman, Steve Greenbaum, Ed Kelley, Pat Gallaher, Dr. Werner Barkhuizen, and Ben Carson Jr.

To my hometown buddies Bub, Ev, Red, Erik, Bos, Wray, Paul, Flav, Kurt, Marsiglio, Keith, Mark, Danny, and the Doctor O'Connell, and my co-conspirator Skyler.

And finally, thank YOU, the entrepreneur, who is ready to start and now must only decide what to do next.

ABOUT THE AUTHOR

JEFF DUDAN is a seasoned business builder, Undercover Boss, and former college football player. He went to Florida to help with recovery in the wake of Hurricane Andrew and two years later launched AdvantaClean, a national restoration franchise that had 240 locations in 37 states when Jeff exited the company in 2019. He's since joined up with his ex-NFL CFO brother, Mike, to start Dudan Partners, a catalyst for enterprise growth in the franchise industry. Jeff recently retired from coaching his kids' sports teams—thirty combined seasons in the past twelve years—and is a top Forbes contributor.

CPSIA information can be obtained
at www.ICGtesting.com
Printed in the USA
LVHW090227100820
662779LV00005B/25/J

9 781544 508528